All Glory to

𐤄 𐤅 𐤄 𐤉
He   Vav   He   Yod
5   6   5   10

Above is the name of God (YHVH) written in PreCannanite Hebrew.

Let me boldly state,
it is the original PreFlood language
of Earth. Or, perhaps better stated,
"The Tongue of Angels & Men."

Satan's Systems, the Great God Nothing,
Prince of the Air, King of Demons
Ruler of Devils...
His Systems are all Broken Towers to Nowhere...
They are Upside Down...
The Most Evil have Ruled Your World
Since the Beginning, even to this Very Day.
What I am Telling you is this:
That the "Knowledge and Wisdom"
of the Ancient Past has been served up
like Raw Sewage on Silver Platters
by the

THUGS

of History.

This Little Book aims to Change that.

In a World of Lies, the Truth becomes
the Most Valuable Thing.
~ Trey Smith

Table of Contents

1) Blood-Lines
page 5

2) The Two Trees ~ Light & Darkness
page 15

3) Tower of Babel
page 24

4) Signs
page 34

5) The War of Noah
page 46

6) Enmerkar & the Lord of Aratta
page 53

7) Abraham & the Fire of Nimrod
page 64

8) Abraham: The Fight of Faith
page 72

Book Layout
Anthony & Laura Winkler

Written, Researched, Graphics & Design by
Trey Smith

BLOOD-LINES
FROM THE FLOOD

Noah → Shem → Abraham
Noah → Japheth
Noah → Ham → Cush → Nimrod/EnMerkar

The Three sons of Noah.

One path leads to the Christ.

The other path, to the AntiChrist.

And, the End begins at the proper place ~
It begins at the New Beginning.

Chapter One

Blood-Lines

NIMROD

The First King of Earth, Post Flood

8 Cush (the son of Ham, the cursed son of Noah) was the father of Nimrod, who became a mighty warrior on the earth. 9 He was a mighty hunter before the Lord; (Proper translation is "Mighty Hunter Against the Lord") that is why it is said, "Like Nimrod, a mighty hunter "Against" the Lord." 10 The first centers of his kingdom were Babylon (Ancient City of Babylone that would become Babylon), Uruk, Akkad (the Assyrian Capitol) and Kalneh, in Shinar ~ Genesis 10:8-10

Tongue Tower Ziggurat in ancient city of Birs-Nimrud (Birs-Nimrod). This is NOT to be confused with the actual ancient city of Nimrud (Nimrod); which was a mesmerizing city of the ancient world named after Nimrod.

Nor is this the actual "Tower of Babel," though it is in the "Babel Governorate."

It is a ziggurat that can be viewed as a memorial to Babel, located just a few miles from ancient Babylon (originally founded by Nimrod).

This ziggurat is dedicated to the god Marduk, whom we will see more clearly later is actually Nimrod's wicked son.

Ancient Ziggurat of Ur

This is a Ziggurat Restored by Saddam Hussein. It is in the Ancient City of Ur which was founded by Nimrod in Modern Day Iraq.

Ur is located near Uruk and Eridu and is also the Birthplace of Abraham.

Statue of King Gilgamesh holding a Pet Lion. Gilgamesh ruled Uruk (seen beneath) following the subduing of Nimrod, and death of Nimrod's son Mardon (later called the god "Marduk").

Gilgamesh claimed he was two parts god and one part man.

Blessings And Curses of the Three Sons

20 Now Noah, a man of the soil, proceeded to plant a vineyard. 21 But when he drank some of its wine, he became drunk and uncovered himself inside his tent. 22 And Ham, the father of Canaan, saw his father's nakedness and told his two brothers outside.

23 Then Shem and Japheth took a **GARMENT** and placed it across their shoulders, and walking backward, they covered their father's nakedness. Their faces were turned away so that they did not see their father's nakedness.

24 When Noah awoke from his drunkenness and learned what his youngest son had done to him, 25 he said,

"Cursed be Canaan! A servant of servants shall he be to his brothers."

Coverings given to Adam & Eve

Adam → Noah

COVERINGS

Noah → Shem → Abraham
Noah → Japheth
Noah → Ham → Cush → Nimrod/EnMerkar
Ham → Canaan (Father of Canaanites)

26 He also declared: "Blessed be the LORD, the God of Shem! May Canaan be the servant of Shem.

27 May God expand the territory of Japheth; may he dwell in the tents of Shem,

and may Canaan be his servant!"

28 After the flood, Noah lived 350 years. 29 So Noah lived a total of 950 years, and then he died.

Note: The curse is technically on Canaan; but the shame for many generations falls on the line of Ham.

The Book of Jasher clarifies these are the garments given to Adam & Eve.

GENESIS 3

21 The Lord God made garments of skin for Adam and his wife and clothed them.

This was the first sacrifice. Something would have to give its skin for the covering of sins.

These "skins" would be important later.

22 And the Lord God said, "The man has now become like one of us, knowing good and evil. He must not be allowed to reach out his hand and take also from the tree of life and eat, and live forever"

23 So the Lord God banished them from the Garden of Eden to work the ground from which he had been taken.

24 After he drove the man out: He placed on the east side of the Garden of Eden cherubim and a flaming sword (represents "Truth") flashing back and forth to guard the way to the tree of life.

"I Am the Way, the Truth, and the Life." ~Jesus

Genesis 3

21 The Lord God made garments of skin for Adam and his wife and clothed them.

Adam → Noah
Coverings

This was the first sacrifice; a symbol that there would be a price for the covering of sins.

Jesus would be the Adam that did not fail, the last sacrifice covering sins.

Jesus came through the bloodline of Shem.

Jasher 3

14 And it was in the fifty-sixth year of the life of Lamech when Adam died; nine hundred and thirty years old was he at his death, and his two sons, with Enoch and Methuselah his son, buried him with great pomp, as at the burial of kings, in the cave which God had told him.

Notes: Methuselah died at 969, the oldest living man.

His name means: "His death shall bring" (the judgment). He died seven days before the flood.

To God, a day is as a thousand years. No-one lived over 1000 yrs.

"In the day you eat of the tree, you shall die."

Methuselah - the oldest living tree in the world, in Bristlecone Pine Forest 4849 years old

Shin 300

Shem is the hidden name for God.

Jasher 7

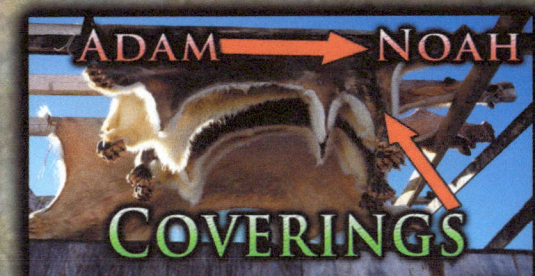

Ancient City of Nimrud (Nimrod) in image

Adam → Noah Coverings

23 And Cush the son of Ham, the son of Noah, took a wife in those days in his old age, and she bare a son, and they called his name Nimrod, saying, At that time the sons of men again began to rebel and transgress against God, and the child grew up, and his father loved him exceedingly, for he was the son of his old age.

Genesis 9

20 Now Noah, proceeded to plant a vineyard. 21 But when he drank some of its wine, he became drunk and uncovered himself inside his tent. 22 And Ham, the father of Canaan, saw his father's nakedness and told his two brothers outside.

24 And the garments of skin which God made for Adam and his wife, when they went out of the garden, were (deceptively) given to Cush. 25 For after the death of Adam and his wife, the garments were given to Enoch, the son of Jared, and when Enoch was taken up to God, he gave them to Methuselah, his son.

26 And at the death of Methuselah, Noah took them and brought them to the ark, and they were with him until he went out of the ark. 27 And in their going out, Ham stole those garments from Noah his father, and he took them and hid them from his brothers.

28 And when Ham begat his firstborn Cush, he gave him the garments in secret, and they were with Cush many days. 29 And Cush also concealed them from his sons and brothers, and when Cush had begotten Nimrod, he gave him those garments through his love for him, and Nimrod grew up, and when he was twenty years old he put on those garments.

30 And Nimrod became strong when he put on the garments.

23 Then Shem and Japheth took a garment and placed it across their shoulders, and walking backward, they covered their father's nakedness. Their faces were turned away so that they did not see their father's nakedness.

24 When Noah awoke from his drunkenness and learned what his youngest son (Ham) had done to him, 25 Noah said,

"Cursed be Canaan! A servant of servants shall he be to his brothers."

Ancient Mesopotamia
Where Life started again after the Flood

Noah
Mt. Ararat

Nineveh → *City of Nimrud is next to Nineveh*

Babylone → *Later Babylon*

Kish (Cush) →

Uruk → *Where Gilgamesh ruled The First City in the World*

Ur → *Where Abraham was born*

Tigris & Euphrates Rivers

Ziggurat of Eridu
Tower of Babel

Egypt

Red Sea

Ancient Population Growth

As you can see above, the First Cities of the Ancient World drop directly down from Mount Ararat; Where Lord Aratta (Noah) lived according to the Bible, Manetho the Historian of Egypt, and Enmerkar (Nimrod) in his Ancient writings.

World populations grow rapidly. If one family has 5 children, and those children have 5 children, and those 5, etc, etc, etc... You come to 10 million people in roughly 10 generations (or the time Abraham was born). By the Time Abraham was 40, it would have both likely & easily doubled to 20 million (at least).

NOAH
A Trey Smith project

Ancient Timeline

You have Six Ages of Empires beginning with the Tiny Sumerian/Assyrian settlements & Temples that begin to sprout up along the Tigris and Euphrates in Modern Day Iraq.

At the Death of Jesus, your Empires turn into religions.

Rome was never conquered. Its Bureaucracy became so large it collapsed in on itself... And today is called the Roman Catholic Church.

Therefore, some call this Time-Period "Rome-Phase II."

3300-2400BC

Pre-Flood → Flood → Nimrod ~ Sumerians → Assyrians → Egyptians → Babylonians → Persians → Greeks → Romans

Determining the date of the Flood is not as simple as it might seem. The exact date of the flood can change depending on the method of the mathematics used, the text used (Septuagint, Masoretic, or Samaritan), the calculations in Genesis 5 and 11 (and interpretation thereof), and the time each generation birthed children in those genealogies.

As strange as it may seem, the dates closer to 2400 BC can mathematically have a shockingly nice fit, particularly when we look at how "stretched" the modern Egyptian timelines are. And, as we learned earlier, population growth happens rapidly... Accordingly, in those days, families were breeding their own little armies of children.

But, a "tight fit" does not necessarily mean a "Right Fit." We lay that in your hands. A general non-precise, rough date for the Flood could be said to be in the ballpark of 3000 BC.

ENOCH
SCRIBE OF RIGHTEOUSNESS

"MUŠHUŠŠU"
THE HYBRID PET DRAGON
OF NIMROD'S SON
SEEN IN IMAGE
FROM BABYLON

WAS BROUGHT IN BEFORE THIS CAST OF FALLEN ANGELS THAT HAD PLAYED "GOD" WITH MANKIND. THE FALLEN ANGELS, DEMONS & THEIR OFFSPRING WOULD LATER BE WORSHIPPED AS GODS. THEY KNEW ENOCH HAD A RELATIONSHIP WITH THE TRUE GOD ~ THUS THEY FEARED HIM.

"AND HEAL THE EARTH WHICH THE ANGELS HAVE CORRUPTED, AND PROCLAIM THE HEALING OF THE EARTH, THAT THEY MAY HEAL... AND THAT ALL THE CHILDREN OF MEN MAY NOT PERISH THROUGH ALL THE SECRET THINGS THAT THE WATCHERS HAVE DISCLOSED AND HAVE TAUGHT THEIR SONS." ~ ENOCH 10

THEY ASKED HIM TO MAKE PRAYERS FOR THEIR FORGIVENESS. THIS WAS GOD'S RESPONSE:

"YOU THOUGHT YOU HAD **SECRETS** YET ALL THE MYSTERIES HAD NOT YET BEEN REVEALED TO YOU, LITTLE DID YOU KNOW, YOU ONLY KNEW THE **WORTHLESS ONES.** YOU SHALL HAVE NO PEACE FOR ALL ETERNITY." ~ ENOCH 16

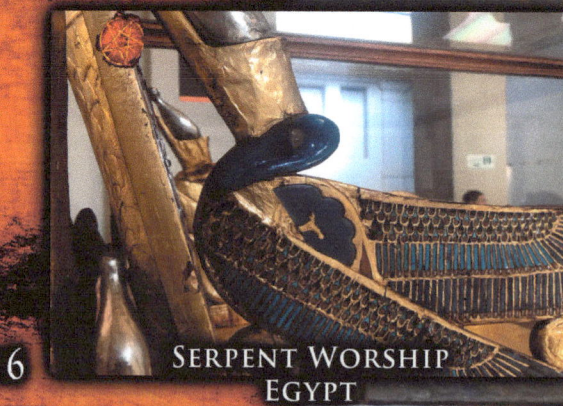

SERPENT WORSHIP
EGYPT

Abram — Shem  — Noah
10 from Noah — 300

The Two Trees

CHAPTER TWO

Light & Darkness

Noah
├── Shem
└── Ham
    ├── Canaan
    ├── Put
    ├── Egypt — also called Mitzraim, or Aegyptus ~ founder of Egypt per Manetho, and Bible
    │   └── King Anom, son of Aegyptus per Jasher 7:11. Later known as the Egyptian god "Amun-Ra"
    │   └── Oswiris the son of King Anom per Jasher 14:2. Later known as the god "Osiris"
    │   └── Rikayon (First Official "Pharaoh"~ probably also the same as Pharaoh Narmer of Dynasty 1) per decree of King Osiris. Rikayon was a tomb saleman, thus the giant tombs in Egypt. Swindles Osiris out of control of Egypt, then charges tax to the people to get to god Osiris in Underworld for answer of prayers.
    └── Cush
        └── Nimrod (also called Sumerian "Enmerkar") Nimrod lived 215 years. He lived at the same time as Abraham. Infact, the Tower of Babel was built while Abram (Abraham) was living in the mountains with Noah and Shem, before Abram was 40 years old and left to visit his father, Terah (Nimrod's head idol maker).

Matthew 24

37 But as the days of Noah were, so also shall the coming of the Son of man be.

Neph Children

Peru

Genesis 6

When men began to multiply on the face of the earth, and daughters were born to them, the sons of God (Angels) saw that they were fair; and they took wives for themselves of all that they chose.

Then the Lord said, "My spirit shall not abide in mortals forever, for they are flesh; their days shall be one hundred twenty years."

The Nephilim were on the earth in those days—and also afterward—when the sons of God (Fallen Angels) went into the daughters of men, who bore children to them. These were the heroes that were of old, warriors of renown.

— Genesis 6:1-4

Nephilim After the Flood

There is some debate about how Nephilim would arise after the flood. Genesis (6) six clearly states they were on the earth after the flood. Additionally, Numbers 13:33 says they later inhabited Canaan at the time of the Israelite conquest of Canaan.

There are suggestions that Nephilim blood could have been on Noah's Ark. Or, in one of the son's wives. However, if God went to such great lengths to ensure every animal was clean, it would be difficult to believe God did not have his hand on all eight of the Ark's passengers.

Following the flood, we see it is the wickedness of mankind coming forth ~ particularly through the linage of Noah's son Ham ~ leading to Egypt, Canaan, and Nimrod.

The use of witchcraft, summons of demons, and the following of the same rituals as before the flood begins at the Tower of Babel.

We have clear Sumerian records, such as the Sumerian "*Enmerkar and Lord Aratta*" stating boldly that mankind was deliberately calling in devils for the purpose of breeding abominations (such as Tammuz) in occult ceremonies much after the flood.

Jasher: Chapter Two

3 And it was in the (Pre-Flood) days of Enosh (not Enoch) that the sons of men continued to rebel and transgress against God, to increase the anger of the Lord against the sons of men.

4 And the sons of men went and they served other gods, and they forgot the Lord who had created them in the earth: and in those days the sons of men made images of brass and iron, wood and stone, and they bowed down and served them.

5 And every man made his own god and they bowed down to them, and the sons of men forsook the Lord all the days of Enosh and his children; and the anger of the Lord was kindled on account of their works and abominations which they did in the earth.

11 And Cainan (son of Enosh) was a very wise man (in ways of evil), and with his wisdom he ruled also over the world of spirits and demons.

ENKI
"Lord of Earth"

Enki is being summonsed. The water wiggly lines represent the Abzu; a portal to the Underworld. Enki's raven is at his side. The "witch hat" is really a symbol for the false Tree of Life.

FALL OF ANGELS

Enki comes forth from a creature called "Tiamat" who is the feminine form of the God of Chaos, and also the Dragon.

Enki is summonsed often by Enmerkar (Nimrod) in Sumerian texts, after the Flood.

Long Life Spans and Giants
The Past is Stranger Than You Thought

Dr. Jack Cuozzo

SKELETON OF GIANT FOUND AT JUNIPER
JULY 26, 1911

Chemung's Predecessors Huge Giants Were Seven Feet Tall and Had Horns
WEDNESDAY, JULY 12, 1916.
A QUEER FELLOW
One of the Most Remarkable Scientific Discoveries in History Made Here—Sixty-eight Skeletons of Men Living 700 Years Ago Unearthed Between Sayre and Waverly—Men Were Old at Forty.

FRIDAY, JULY 11, 1919.
A GIANT SKELETON EIGHTEEN FEET TALL

AUSTIN, Tex., June 14.—"If the report that the fossilized skeleton of a giant eighteen feet tall has been found near Seymour, Tex., is true, it is the most important ethnological discovery ever made in the world," remarked Dr. J. E. Pearce, professor of anthropology of the University of Texas. "It would break all previous records of giants by nearly ten feet, as the tallest man known to anthropological research was only eight feet inches in height."
The skeleton is in possession of W. McKinney, Houston, Tex., oil prospector, who found it, and has been seen by a number of people who vouch for the truth of the size of the relic of a heretofore unknown race.
Mr. McKinney, while making an excavation on the narrow watershed between the Brazos and Wichita rivers, came upon the fossilized skeleton near the surface. Mr. Kinney writes:
"I estimate that this man weighed from two thousand to twenty-five hundred pounds. According to my deductions he lived about twenty-eight hundred years ago. The skull is six times the size of that of an ordinary man."
Mr. McKinney does not explain how he arrived at the figures...

Flinders Petrie, 1903
Famed Egyptologist

Neanderthals are extremely tough human skeletons that lived extraordinarily long lives. As we covered in *"Preflood."*

Above, Dr. Jack Cuozzo holds a Neanderthal skull. He was the first to scientifically discover these were humans living hundreds of years.

Humans were larger, in every respect.

ELEVEN FEET TALL
Skeletons of Prehistoric Giants earthed in Michigan Mounds
A Carson City (Mich.) correspondent of the Detroit News writes that the mains of a forgotten race were dug up from the mounds on the side of Crystal lake, Montcalm...

A NEW RACE HAS BEEN FOUND...THESE STRANGE REMAINS ARE FOUND OVER MORE THAN A HUNDRED MILES OF COUNTRY, FROM ABYDOS TO GEBELEN.
THE RACE WAS VERY TALL AND POWERFUL, WITH STRONG FEATURES: A HOOKED NOSE, LONG POINTED BEARD, AND BROWN WAVY HAIR, ARE SHOWN BY THEIR CARVINGS AND BODILY REMAINS. ~ FLINDERS PETRIE

Human Skeletons
Neanderthal
Modern Man — Ancient Man

Robert Wadlow ~ Tallest Man

Wadlow's shoe, provided by Brent Biddle (to Trey's right), is a size "37."
Robert Wadlow was just shy of nine (9) feet tall.
Is to be noted that just because an individual has "unusual features" does NOT mean they have demon, angel or Nephilim blood.

But, it could mean they have traits which are a throwback to ancient times.

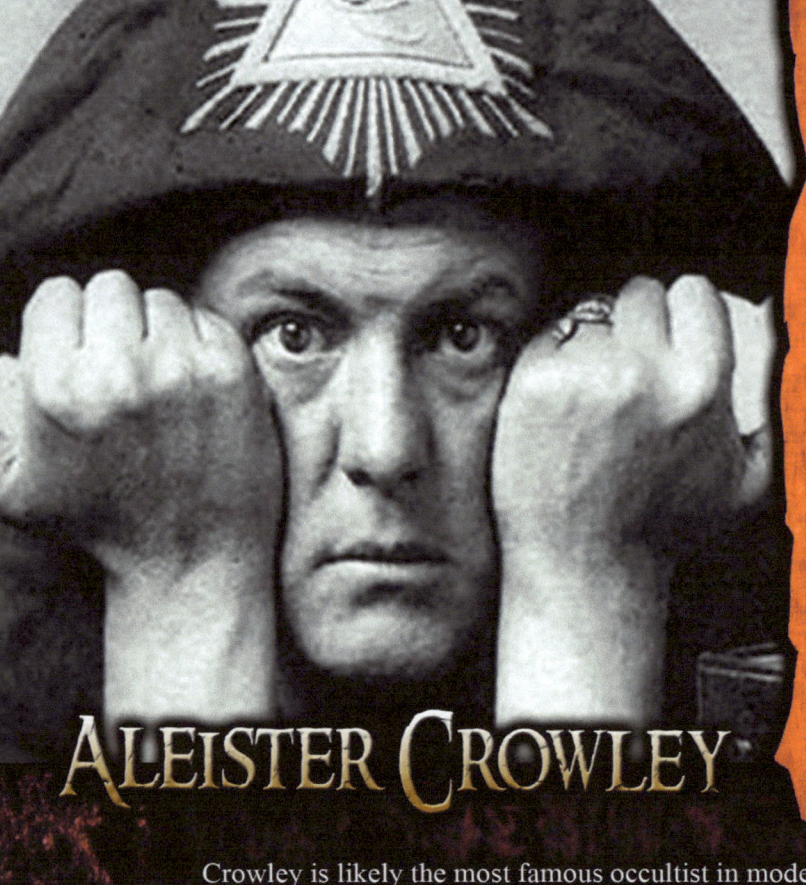

ALEISTER CROWLEY

AYIN 70

The "Ayin" is the number 70 in ancient Hebrew. It is the symbol one would expect to find leading to the end-times.

And, also the symbol for Daniel's 70th week, or the revelation week.

The Ayin is a powerful symbol for God, but can be and is copied by the demonic.

Ayin, (as with the "Alef") is a silent letter. The Ayin is said to "SEE" but "not speak."

It represents the Light of God from Genesis 1:3

However, if the eye be the "evil-eye" (Ayin Ra) then "How great it's garkness" ~ Matt 6:22-23

CROWLEY'S DEMON GUIDE "LAM"

THE WAY

LAM is the Tibetan word for Way or Path, and LAMA is He who Goeth, the specific title of the Gods of Egypt, the Treader of the Path, in Buddhistic phraseology.   Its numerical value is 71, the number of this book.

Crowley is likely the most famous occultist in modern history, living from 1875 to 1947.

He was also a highly recognized 33 Degree Freemason, and high member of witchy secret societies such as the Golden Dawn.

The image to the right is a dimensional entity he called, Lam.

Crowley did ceremonies involving drinking of blood, goats, and sacrifice.

This entity "Lam" he claimed would physically manifest in the midst of some of these rituals.

It is also believed to be the first drawing in modern history of what is called a: Gray Alien.

"Today they call them angels and demons, tomorrow they will call them something else" ~ famous Crowley Quote

LAM, THE ALIEN LOOKING CHARACTER ABOVE, WAS CLAIMED BY CROWLEY TO TRAVEL WITH ANOTHER ENTITY CALLING ITSELF "AIWASS."

AIWASS WAS SAID TO BE A DIMENSIONAL ANCIENT ASSYRIAN KING, THAT CROWLEY DESCRIBED AS: "FACE OF A SAVAGE KING, AND EYES VEILED LEST THEIR GAZE SHOULD DESTROY WHAT THEY SAW... MY (CROWLEY'S) PERSONAL ANGEL." ~ ALEISTER CROWLEY

THE CROW

Nimrod's Wicked Son "Mardon," or later god "Marduk." His Pet Dragon in boat. Name Marduk means: Son of Utu (Ham).

MARDUK
BORN FROM THE ENKI

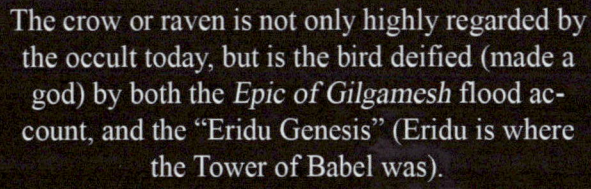

ENKI

STEPPING THROUGH PORTAL OF ABYSS WITH CROW.

MANLY P. HALL
33RD DEGREE FREEMASON

IMAGE SOURCE: "An Encyclopedic Outline of Masonic, Hermetic, Quabbalist and Rosicrucian Symbolical Philosophy."

The crow or raven is not only highly regarded by the occult today, but is the bird deified (made a god) by both the *Epic of Gilgamesh* flood account, and the "Eridu Genesis" (Eridu is where the Tower of Babel was).

"Noah opened a window he had made in the ark and sent out a raven, and it kept flying to and fro" (it was a worthless bird) ~ Genesis 8

Now, if we look in Job 1:6 it says:

6 The bene-ha elohim (angels) came to present themselves before the Lord, and Satan was amongst them. 7 The Lord said to Satan, "Where have you come from?"

Satan answered the Lord, "From roaming throughout the earth, going to and fro on it."

BLACK MAGICIAN ELIPHAS LEVI IS PICTURED ABOVE USING A "GRIMOIRE" (BOOK OF RITUAL MAGICK).

HE HAS OPENED A PORTAL TO THE DARK WORLD TO SUMMON AN ANCIENT WISDOM DEMON CALLED A "YODA."

THE OCCULT HAS BELIEVED SINCE THE BEGINNING THAT DEMONIC ENTITIES ARE REAL,

AND, THAT THEY CAN MANIFEST.

THESE ENTITIES NOT ONLY HATE YOU, THEY WISH THEY COULD BE YOU.

~ TREY SMITH

ANSWERS IN GENESIS ARK ReCREATION

Noah's Ark was NOT just a literal event in the history of our world. It is also a symbolism from God to man.

13 "Enter through the narrow gate. For wide is the gate and broad is the road that leads to destruction, and many enter through it.

14 But small is the gate and narrow the road that leads to life, and only a few find it."

~ Matthew 7

NOAH'S ARK

LIKE THE TWO TREES IN THE GARDEN, OR TWO PATHS, THE OCCULT HAS FAVORED THE RAVEN, THE FALCON, THE CROW...

WHILST GOD FAVORS THE DOVE.

THE DOVE RETURNED WITH AN OLIVE BRANCH IN ITS MOUTH TO NOAH ON THE BOAT.

THE DOVE IS A SYMBOL OF HOPE, THE SPIRIT OF GOD, PEACE, FREEDOM, AND ALSO ISRAEL.

THE RAVEN IS A SYMBOL OF DARKNESS AND BONDAGE.

THE RAVEN

EYE OF HORUS

HORUS
Part man/part god, birthed from dead god Osiris & Isis. He is also the symbol of the raven from the boat.

GARUDA
Bird of Lord Vishnu. Lord Vishnu is king of air, where he rules from his bed of naga serpents.

THE DOVE
LUKE 3:21-23

21 When all the people were being baptized, Jesus was baptized too.

And as He was praying, heaven was opened, 22 and the Holy Spirit descended on Him in a bodily form like a dove.

And a voice came from heaven: "You are My beloved Son; in You I am well pleased." 23 Jesus Himself was about thirty years old when He began His ministry.

NOAH → SHEM

Genesis 11

Genesis 11:10 records that Shem was 100 years old at the birth of Arphaxad, two years after the flood. He lived for another 500 years after this, making his age at death 600 years.

None of the three (3) sons were little children as is commonly depicted.

Shem, the oldest son, was a hundred years old, when he begat his first son Arpachshad, two years after the flood.

Shem's son Arpachshad lived five and thirty years, and begot Shelah. 13 And Shelah lived thirty years, and begot Eber. Eber lived four and thirty years, and begot Peleg. Peleg lived thirty years, and begot Reu. Reu lived two and thirty years, and begot Serug. Serug lived thirty years, and begot Nahor. Nahor lived nine and twenty years, and begot Terah...

Terah ~ The Head Idol Maker for Nimrod ~ lived **seventy years, and begot Abram** (Abraham).

Through Abraham Comes Israel.

Shem: from the birth of Arphaxad (Shem's son), two years after the flood, until the birth of Abram, it was only 292 years. Noah lived 350 years after the flood and Shem 500 years.

Abram's life overlapped Noah's life by 58 years.

58 is the number of grace.

NUN 50 + **CHET 8** ⬜ = REST GRACE NOAH

If you multiply 50 x 8 = 400.

And, 400 is the Tav, the cross.

✝ TAV 400

Noah was Abraham's great, great, great, great, great, great, great, great-grandfather.

Abraham only lived to be 175, so Shem actually outlived Abraham by 35 years.

Abraham, Noah, Shem & Nimrod all lived at the same overlapping time.

Enoch 10:11 And the Lord said unto Michael: 'Go, bind Semjaza and his fallen angels... bind them fast for **seventy generations** in the valleys of the earth, till the Day of the Last Judgment.

70 → Seventy in Hebrew means judgment & sacrifice ~ it means both light and dark.

> "WHEN THE KINGSHIP WAS LOWERED FROM HEAVEN, THE KINGSHIP WAS IN ERIDU."
> ~SUMERIAN KING'S LIST

TOWER OF BABEL
THE ZIGGURAT OF ERIDU

THE BASE OF THE TOWER OF BABEL, SEEN TO THE RIGHT, IS ROUGHLY 25 ACRES, OR 20 FOOTBALL FIELDS.

THE CITY EXPANDED OUTWARD FOR MILES. IT WAS LOCATED RIGHT NEXT DOOR TO NIMROD'S OCCULT CITIES OF URUK AND UR.

ONLY THE BASE REMAINS.

THIS TOWER WAS DEDICATED TO THE ENKI.

IT WAS CALLED, "THE GATEWAY FOR THE GOD."

AMARNA, SEEN IN IMAGE, WAS THE LIKELY THE LARGEST TEMPLE PALACE IN EGYPT (OUTSIDE KARNAK). YOU CAN SEE THE MASSIVE BASE, YET ALL THAT REMAINS ARE THESE TWO PILLARS.

THE MAMMOTH STONES WERE USED OVER TIME FOR OTHER PROJECTS, JUST LIKE THE STONES OF THE TOWER OF BABEL.

Manetho

The secular education world has chosen to use Manetho, a priest of both Thoth and Marduk, who lived at the time of the Greeks in the 3rd century BC, for their Egyptian history, upon which they have based World History.

You will often hear it said that Egyptian history is "rock-solid" in its Timelines. Nothing could further from Reality.

The Truth is: They have pulled what they like from Manetho's "Aegyptiaca" History and ignored the Rest. Manetho does however do us grand favors by matching the Egyptian Gods with the Greek gods; like a Rosetta Stone of Demons & Devils. By "Golden Age of gods" (not to be confused with the "Golden Age of Prosper" for Egypt following Joseph) they are referring to a mixture of events slightly before and after the Flood.

Additionally, you will notice that Manetho's history, clearly filtered through Nimrod & Sumeria, with a twist of knowledge from books like Enoch, is actually telling the Biblical story.

Manetho's Aegyptiaca (History of Egypt)

5 Mestraim (matches with Genesis 10) lived not long after the Flood. For after the Flood, Cham (or Ham), son of Noah, begat Aegyptus or Mestraim, who was the first to set out to establish himself in Egypt, at the time when the tribes began to disperse this way and that (following Babel). Now the whole time from Adam to the Flood was 2242 years.

12 The Zodiac has an equal number of parts, 360 (this comes from Enoch's Calendar). So, it came to pass that the reigns of the gods who ruled among them for six generations in six dynasties (structured in lots of sets of six just like the Sumerian King's List).

Manetho's "Golden Age of Gods"

1. Hêphaestus (Ptah) for 727¾ years.
2. Hêlios (Ra the, Sun), for 80 years.
3. Agathodaemôn, for 56 7/12 years.
4. Cronos (Saturn/Enki), for 40 years.
5. Osiris and Isis, for 35 years.
6. Typhon, for 29 years.
7. Orus, for 20 years.
8. Ares, for 23 years.
9. Anubis, 17 years.
10. Hercules, for 15 years.
11. Apollo, for 25 years.
12. Ammon, for 30 years.
13. Tithoes, for 27 years.
14. Sosus, for 32 years.
15. Zeus (represents Marduk, son of Enki, Jupiter), for 20 years.

Sumerian King's List

The 12 Months used for man's "gods"
JUPITER & SATURN

MARDUK

Though Planets are Creations of God, the Empires began Worshiping them as Their Demon Gods.

Jupiter, in the Occult, is the Son of Saturn, or the Son of Satan. Accordingly, Saturn is also the Sixth (6) Planet.

Jupiter is the Sumerian Planet Symbol for the god Marduk.

The Sumerian "Mul.Apin I" states: "One Big (Wandering) Star ~ that is Marduk, Nibiru, the Wandering Star Jupiter (One of many examples).

Later, for the Romans and Greeks "Marduk" had become "Zeus."

UnHoly Trinity

SEMIRAMIS also called "Inanna," The Moon Goddess.

NIMROD also called "Enmerkar." Summonsed Enki.

TAMMUZ the goat king. part man / part god. Reared by Nimrod, born by Enki.

Enki in the Ancient Sumerian Occult is Saturn (Satan).

ENKI

Is Symbolized by Saturn just as the Later Greek & Roman Cronos became "Saturn."

ZEUS For the Romans and Greeks he was the Planet Jupiter Son of Saturn (Greek god Cronos).

The Mythologies have been Telling you Occult history. The Golden Age of the Gods was the Time of Fallen Angels and Devils before the Flood.

CRONOS For the Romans and Greeks was the Product of Uranus.

GILGAMESH & ENKIDU

In the Sumerian King's List, Enmerkar (Nimrod) is named as the first king following the flood. The "Kar" in the name "Enmerkar" means: "The Hunter" ~ just as the Bible calls Nimrod: "the Mighty Hunter."

Enmerkar also founded the exact same Cities in the Sumerian writings as Nimrod founded in the Biblical account. Those cities are: Babylon, Uruk, Akkad, Kalneh, and the grand temple to the god Enki in Eridu (known also as the Tower of Babel) in Shinar.

Enmerkar is technically proceeded in the Sumerian King's list by Meskiagkasher (the Biblical Cush), Utu (the Biblical Ham), and finally Utnapishtim (the Biblical Noah). They are in that order perfectly, in Sumerian, just as the Bible lists them in Hebrew.

Both Enkidu and Gilgamesh are listed as the Third and Fourth (or Fourth and Fifth) Kings of Uruk according to the Sumerian King's List. Both were friends, and actually ruled and took journeys together at the same time.

Enkidu's name means: Created by the Enki.

The Sumerian King's list calls Enkidu: "Dumuzid." And, Dumuzid would later become the word "Tammuz" ~ the part man, part goat creature. Depicted in the *Epic of Gilgamesh*.

Enkidu is the product of Semiramis (also called "Inanna" or "Ishtar") ~ the Lust Goddess. She is also Nimrod's wife, and this "Goat-Man" was birthed by a "Sex-Magic" Ritual with the Enki. So, the Enkidu (Tammuz) is not only the Abomination son of Nimrod's wife, but is also intimate with Nimrod's Wife (this creature's own mother, birthed by the Devil).

Note: Nimrod's real son, between Nimrod and Inanna (Semiramis), is "Mardon," who dies in battle. This "goat-man" abomination, Enkidu (Tammuz, later called the "god Pan"), is claimed by the Sumerians themselves to be the product of some type of intense sex ritual where the Enki impregnates Nimrod's (Enmerkar's) wife.

According to the *Epic of Gilgamesh*, Gilgamesh befriends Enkidu by letting this Goat-Man ravage the "Temple Prostitutes."

Then, Gilgamesh and Enkidu go to hunt a creature called "Humbaba," who the text says was raised by "Utu" (Noah's cursed son Ham). The creature they go hunt is said to be Mammoth & enormous in size and has: "...a body covered in thorny scales; his feet had the claws of a vulture, and on his head were giant horns... his tail like that of a snake. Roar is as a flood"

Humbaba is likely some type of Dinosaur / Dragon. They do find it and kill it in a Cedar Forest.

When Enkidu (the Goat-Man) dies, Gilgamesh does an Occult ceremony for which it states a portal opens and the spirit of Enkidu (the Goat) comes through. The text about the Underworld is strangely missing, but it is clear Enkidu tells Gilgamesh it is a VERY BAD place.

Gilgamesh seeks out Utnapishtim (Noah) to find out about the Tree of Life. Noah's wife tells him it might be under the deep waters somewhere. Gilgamesh then claims he finds (what he believes to be) a piece of fruit from the Tree of Life, then a giant Snake takes it from him.

**PAN
ENKIDU
DUMUZID
TAMMUZ**

**Witches' Sabbath
1798**

NOAH
MT. ARARAT

Eridu was founded by the "First King of Earth" (Enmerkar) and grew around a MASSIVE Temple. The homes were made of mud brick and built on top of one another, and Rose upwards and Outwards.

The temple grew upward the larger the city became.

Eridu is called the Oldest City in the World. The Ziggurat Tower at the highest point, the heart of Eridu (Tower of Babel), was the Largest in the World.

Even the Sumerians claim the "gods" destroyed their Tower to the Heavens.

Tigris & Euphrates Rivers — Modern Iraq

Ziggurat of Eridu
Tower of Babel

Ziggurat of Eridu
Tower of Babel

Excerpt from
Enmerkar (Nimrod) & Lord Aratta (Noah)

"Enki, the wise and knowing lord of the Earth, shall bring the speech (worship) in their mouths, so the speech of mankind is truly one."

The Ruins of the Ziggurat of Eridu have been re-built upon many times. The materials for the Destroyed Tower carried off and for other Assyrian/Babylonian cities.

Noah ~ "Utnapishtim" in Epic of Gilgamesh

Also called, "Lord of Aratta" by Enmerkar (Nimrod) for the "Mountains of Ararat" where the boat landed. And, it is the area where Noah lived with his vineyards. It is also called Mount Nisir in the *Epic of Gilgamesh*, which means, "Mountain of Salvation."

Ham (the Cursed Son of Noah) ~ "Utu" in Sumerian

Ham "Utu" also called "Shamash: the sun god"

Utu (the biblical Ham) is the grandfather of Inanna (the first moon goddess). Inanna would become the lust goddess of the occult, taking on titles such as: "Queen of Heaven." She was the granddaughter of Ham (Utu), also the wife of her brother, Nimrod (Enmerkar), and mother of Tammuz (the goat). She also was intimate with her "goat-son." Inanna was regarded so highly by the occult that she was promoted to "twin of Utu" ~ meaning "twin of Noah's cursed son, Ham: who stole the garments of Adam & Eve." This was merely a royal title as Inanna was actually Ham's very spoiled and arrogant favorite granddaughter.

Ham's son, Cush, gets the garments of Adam & Eve in Jasher, following his father, Ham, stealing them from Noah. Cush then has four sons; but in his very old age has a youngest son named "Nimrod." Then, the Sumerian's pick up the story claiming that after the birth of Nimrod and giving him the empire, Cush took a sea journey and did not return. One can only imagine he knew boat building very well ~ and likely took a large staff.

It is true that many of the pyramids and ziggurats around the world, like in South America, look strikingly similar to their counterparts in Egypt, Sumeria, and Babylon.

Whatever the case, the biblical Cush (called Mes-ki-ang-gasher by the Sumerian King's list) gave the garments of Adam and Eve to his youngest son Nimrod. The Book of Jasher calls Nimrod, the son of Cush's old age; meaning Cush was likely over the age 200 when he birthed Nimrod.

Cush (Son of Ham) ~ "Mesh-ki-ang-gasher" in Sumerian

Excerpt from Sumerian King's List: "Meš-ki-aŋ-gašher, (Cush) the son of Utu (Ham), became En (Lordand Lugal (King). He ruled (lived) 324 years. He then entered the sea and disappeared."

Notes: Meš-ki-ang-gašher (Cush, son of Ham) is credited by the Sumerians with building the Temple of E-ana (a Ziggurat Temple to Inanna, his daughter) in Uruk. His son, Enmerkar (Nimrod) was the baby of the family, given rule beginning at the age of 20. Nimrod was young enough when Cush appointed him king to be the son, or grandson even, of his own brothers.

Whereas this first little town of Uruk, and its Temple, would be dedicated to his daughter, Inanna (the Goddess); his favorite son, Enmerkar (Nimrod), would get the Larger prize ~ the garments given by God to Adam & Eve.

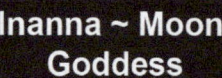

Inanna ~ Moon Goddess

Pyramid of the Moon, Teotihuacán, Mexico

Excerpt from Jasher 7: "Ham stole those garments from Noah his father, and he took them, And when Ham begat his first born, Cush, he gave him the garments in secret, and they were with Cush many days. And when Cush had begotten Nimrod, he gave him those garments through his love for him... the son of his (very) old age."

NIMROD ~ "ENMERKAR" ON SUMERIAN KING'S LIST

Not only does the "Kar" in Enmerkar mean "The Hunter," as well as every city he founded match Tit-for-Tat with the Biblical account ~ but larger still ~ the actual arguments he had with Noah (Lord of Aratta), demanding a blessing for the Tower of Babel itself, is recorded in the Sumerian account of: "Enmerkar and the Lord of Aratta."

It is one of the most treasured documents of Sumeria, and the entire ancient world.

This document is written by Nimrod (Enmerkar) and taken by his best messengers to Noah (Lord of Aratta).

ENMERKAR AND THE LORD OF ARATTA
The Most Prideful & Arrogant Document of the Ancient World

Enmerkar, grandson of Utu (Cursed son Ham), made a plea to his sister, the lady who grants desires, Holy Inanna:

"My sister, let Aratta (Noah, my Great Grandfather) fashion gold and silver skillfully on my behalf... Let Aratta (Noah) build me a temple brought down from heaven -- your place of worship. Let Aratta submit beneath my yoke. Let the people of Aratta bring down for me the mountain stones from their mountain, build the great shrine for me, erect the great abode for me, make the great abode, the abode of the gods, that I may be famed in all the earth!"

And they said, "Come, let us build ourselves a city, and a tower whose top is in the heavens; let us be famed in all the earth." ~ Genesis 11:4

Enmerkar (Nimrod) continues: "May I (Nimrod), the radiant youth, may I be embraced there by you (Noah)!

May Utu (my father Ham, your cursed son) witness it in joy. May (Noah/Aratta) dance around me (Nimrod) in my fields like the Dumuzid (my cursed, abomination son Tammuz, who sleeps with my sister, who is also my wife).

Noah's replies to this occultic and arrogant Sumerian document by Nimrod will be seen in chapter six.

Following the fall and destruction of the Tower of Babel, there are issues where Nimrod tries to kill Abram (Abraham), three times actually, which we will also cover in the coming chapters, after which God stops tolerating Nimrod.

Nimrod, however, is still in charge ~ until he tries to pursue (kill) Abraham for the third time. Three strikes, you're out. It is then that Rebellion rises amongst Nimrod's underling Princes ~ most notably Chedorlaomer of Elam ~ called in Sumerian "Lugalbanda."

JASHER

Jasher 13:15 And all those kings fought there, and Nimrod and his people were smitten before the people of Chedorlaomer, and there fell from Nimrod's men about six hundred thousand, and Mardon the king's son fell amongst them.

13:16 And Nimrod fled and returned in shame and disgrace to his land, and he was (allowed to live in his land) under subjection to Chedorlaomer

NOAH
Mt. Ararat

Nineveh
City of Nimrud is next to Nineveh

Babylone
Later Babylon

Kish (Cush)

Uruk
Where Gilgamesh ruled The First City in the World

Elam

Ur
Where Abraham was born

Tigris & Euphrates Rivers

Red Sea

Ziggurat of Eridu

Tower of Babel

Artist recreation of Eridu where Tower of Babel was.

Chedorlaomer of Elam ~ "Lugalbanda" on Sumerian King's List

Lugalbanda (Lugal-Banda meaning "King Banda") directly follows Enmerkar (Nimrod) as the next king on the Sumerian King's List. The list says that Enmerkar (lived) ruled for 420 years. However, Jasher places him at 215 years ~ which is mathematically more correct. Either way, this does emphasize the extraordinarily long life of Nimrod, consistent with the long lives of those directly following the flood. Noah's so, Shem, for example lived 600 years, and actually outlived Abraham ~ Noah lived 950 years. The rule of Lugalbanda in the Sumerian King's List says he (lived) ruled 1,200 years ~ it is assumed this is merely to make him look bigger, badder and meaner than Enmerkar (Nimrod) whom he defeated.

Abraham would later kill Chedorlaomer, to save Lot before the destruction of Sodom & Gomorrah.

None-the-Less, in the Sumerian story of "Lugalbanda in the Mountain Cave," and others, Lugalbanda is a prince (from Elam) under Enmerkar (Nimrod) ~ identifying him as one in the same as the biblical Chedorlaomer. "Lugal" in his name means "king."

It is worthy of note, that in these same Sumerian stories, Inanna, the spoiled drama & lust goddess granddaughter of Utu (Ham), is always nagging her brother/husband Enmerkar (Nimrod) to give Noah (Aratta) trouble and put him under submission.

Occult Tammuz ~ "Dumazid" on Sumerian King's List

The names "Enkidu, Tammuz, or Dumazid" all refer to the strange part-man / part-goat creature birthed by Nimrod's (Enmerkar's) wife and sister, Inanna. The name "Enkidu" means "Enki's creation."

Though Nimrod's actual son, Mardon (later called the god "Marduk") dies in battle; this "Enkidu creature" is often referred to as a wild hairy man living in the bush, with horns ~ ravaging the animals, and often depicted intimately with goats. Enkidu would later be called the god Pan ~ and the Baphomet.

Enkidu or Tammuz, according to the *Epic of Gilgamesh*, also is intimate with the temple prostitutes, and Inanna (his own mother).

In fact, it is a temple prostitute of Gilgamesh who is said to "tame" Enkidu. Then bringing him to become a major cult sect in Uruk ~ a town described as a constant orgy of pagan gods.

Marduk

Gilgamesh ~ The Spoiled Rich (Kid) King

Excerpt from *Epic of Gilgamesh* (Tablet One):

"Offspring of Lugalbanda, Gilgamesh is strong to perfection, from the day of birth, "I am King" I was called "Gilgamesh," two-thirds god, one-third man."

Trey's Notes: One can only speculate what that means? I lay that in the reader's hands.

A simple translation could be: Gilgamesh comes from a brood of witches and devils.

Gilgamesh was probably ruling the same lands of Nimrod, under his father Chedorlaomer's true kingship ~ giving Gilgamesh the ability to write his "playboy-like" epics and live his "soap opera" life-style. In fact, the *Epic of Gilgamesh* is likely a reflection, or memoir, on the time period when Nimrod was king, and Gilgamesh's father was the top military commander... and Tammuz & Gilgamesh were childhood friends now in their 30s or 40s.

Sumerian King's List

made simple beneath & matched up with its biblical equivalent. Note that the list technically starts with "Mesh-ki-ang-gasher." Utu is the "father and claimed sun-god" starting the list.

1) **Utu - Biblical Ham**
2) **Mesh-ki-ang-gasher - Biblical Cush**
3) **Enmerkar - Biblical Nimrod**
4) **Lugalbanda - Biblical Chedorlaomer**
5) **Dumuzid - Tammuz (Goat-Man)**
6) **Gilgamesh - Son of Chedorlaomer**

Gilgamesh's visit to Noah (Utnapishtim) for soul searching purposes was probably before the death of Nimrod, and only shortly before the death of Noah ~ and not long after the fall of the Tower of Babel when Eridu's occult was in crisis and chaos.

Chapter Four

Signs

THE STARS

The Seed of Righteousness
And the Seed of Darkness began
to sprout again in
the Earth.

Both had their Signs.

Even the Fallen Angels, later worshipped as "gods," watched the stars. Following the flood, mankind did the same. The Stars tell the Biblical story.

"And God said, 'Let there be lights in the vault of the sky to separate the day from the night, and let them serve as signs to mark sacred times, and days and years,"

Mankind tried to worship the stars, as opposed to the God who created them.

STARS & SIGNS

Mount Hermon has three peaks, borders three countries, and its name means: "Mountain of the Chief."

It was called the "chief mountain" as it was the highest of high places of occult worship.

Mount Hermon is located at 33.33 degrees north, and 33.33 degrees east, based on the Paris 0 meridian.

33.33 also corresponds with one third of the Angels falling.

"And his tail swept away a third of the stars of heaven, and threw them to the earth. And the dragon stood before the woman who was about to give birth, so that when she gave birth he might devour her child,"
~ Rev. 12:4

The Canaanites would pray towards Mt. Hermon to their dark god "Baal (Satan)."

Deuteronomy 3

"The Lord our God helped us destroy King Og and his army... His kingdom had sixty towns... His land stretched from the Arnon River gorge in the south, to Mount Hermon in the north."

King Og was the last of the Rephaim ~ means "Giants" and also "Spirits of the Dead."

King Og's coffin is thirteen and a half feet long and six feet wide." (Made of black stone believed to have fallen from the sky).

In the *Epic of Gilgamesh*, Enkidu (the goat-man Pan, also called Tammuz, or Dumazid) visits Mount Hermon with Gilgamesh as the "earth shakes."

Though Pan would have his own worship and cult, Nimrod's other son ~ Mardon ~ is said to be "more wicked than his father" was also later deified and called "Marduk" in the later empire of Babylon as the main "god."

Much of the ancient occult is the worship of ancestors. This begins with Noah's cursed son Ham (called Utu in Sumerian) being worshipped as the "sun-god" ~ a precursor to the Egyptian sun-god "Ra."

Even though Ham was a worthless thief and liar, he and his children gave themselves grand titles ~ "the Magnificent this" or the "Majestic that" ~ as if to hide their own shame.

They literally birthed the upside-down political systems of the New Occult World Order to rise as the dark phoenix, falcon, raven & crow following the flood.

Even going so far as to call themselves "gods."

GIANT STONE DEDICATED TO THE FALLEN ANGELS ON TOP OF HERMON, WITH PAN'S CAVE AT THE BASE.

36 ← CURIOUS PAGE NUMBER FOR THE SEED OF DARKNESS

STARS

The Word "Star" in the Bible is often referencing Angels.

Gabriel is always affiliated with the coming of the Christ.

I would submit to your hands that the reality of the heavens and stars above is far more interesting than modern science proposes. Further, that whatever those distant lights actually be ~ They have properties that may astound us.

When it says the "wise men" followed a "star" that eventually hovered over the birthplace of Jesus ~ that is indeed an unusual star.

These "wise men" ~ in massive caravans from Persia ~ came bearing three gifts (thus the common depiction of Three Wise Men). Gold is the symbol of kingship on earth, frankincense (an incense) as a symbol of deity, and myrrh (an embalming oil) as a symbol of death.

Daniel a Hebrew interpreter of dreams, as a captive, then top advisor in Babylon (which would later become Persia), was not only visited by Gabriel and given the exact math for the day the Messiah would arrive in Israel ~ but Daniel ran the department of the "wise men." On an interesting note, these wise men could have even been combined with "wise men" from the further east in China.

There is a Legend in China of wise men who followed a star to a "Star Child." Accordingly, the Sanxing wise men (三星 "three stars") are worshipped as household idols, and considered "star gods." The old Christmas Carol goes: "We three kings of orient are..."

The Star of David (seen to the left) is a six-pointed star, representing man. The Rabbis believe it represents the creation week, having the Sabbath, or the Seventh Day, God's day of rest as the hexagon, the portal or doorway in the heart ~ the center.

It is comprised of two triangles ~ like two arrows ~ one pointing up, and one pointing down. As if the plane where man stands is on that "deciding line" ~ six also being the only number (the Vav) in Hebrew which connects heaven to Earth. And, the One who decides the "Up" or "Down" is in the Center, the Heart.

This symbol has been used by both God and the occult alike. There is also a possibility it could have been the very symbol on Goliath's shield. In Genesis 20, Joseph says: "You meant evil against me, but God used it for good." So, in King David's case, by cutting the head from the giant, perhaps God was taking one of His powerful symbols back.

GABRIEL
"GOD IS MY STRENGTH"
ANGEL FOR ISRAEL

37 star in 73 star   37 hexagon in 73 star

The Number 37 is a centered hexagonal number and a star number. The word "wisdom" or "chokmah" in Hebrew can have a gematria of both 37 and 73. 37 and 73 are reflective numbers. 37 and 73 are the 12th and 21st prime numbers, respectively. 12 and 21 are also reflective numbers. 37 is one of the Creator's numbers, a "Star of David" ~ yet, it crosses paths with the Antichrist, just as the "up" and "down" arrows that make the star. 6+6+6=18 and 18 x 37 = 666. Just as in Exodus 1:8 ~ "A pharaoh came that knew not Joseph." Perhaps a foreshadowing that this star has connection in passing with the Antichrist system in the end. I would note that all numbers belong to God, the devil is a thief ~ like Noah's son Ham.

3
(7 7 7)
37

ENOCH

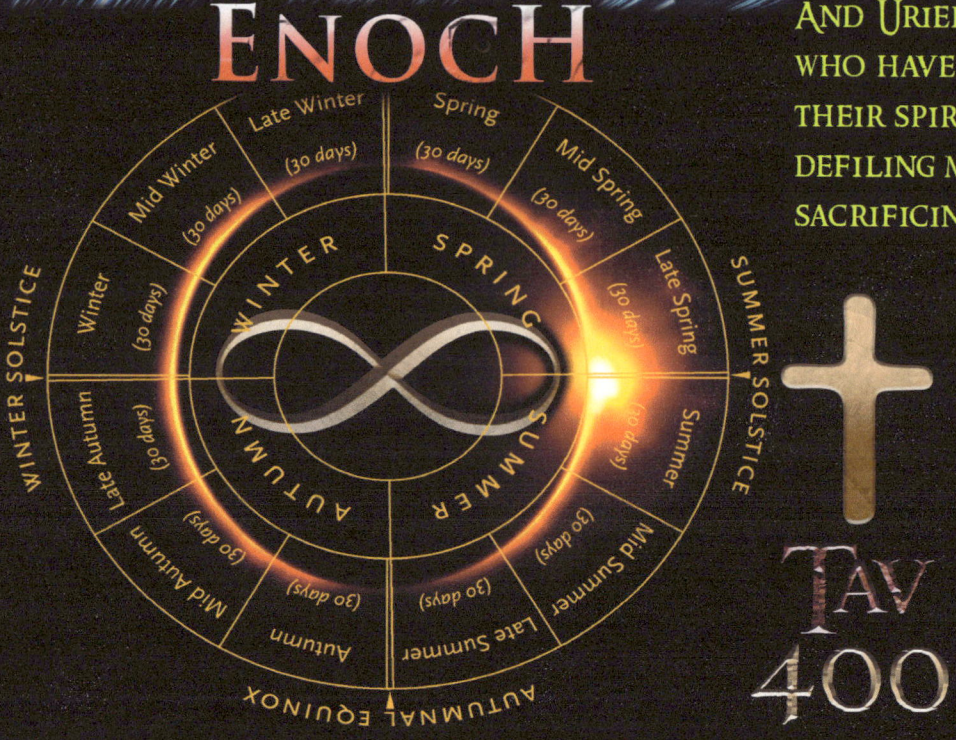

AND URIEL SAID TO ME: "HERE SHALL STAND THE ANGELS WHO HAVE CONNECTED THEMSELVES WITH WOMEN, AND THEIR SPIRITS ASSUMING MANY DIFFERENT FORMS ARE DEFILING MANKIND AND SHALL LEAD THEM ASTRAY INTO SACRIFICING TO DEMONS AS GODS." ~ ENOCH 19:1

✝ TAV 400

The Book of Enoch is divided into five (the number of grace) major sections. The Book of the Heavenly Luminaries (where Uriel gives Enoch the Calendar) is in section III.

Enoch's Calendar is the basis for every ancient calendar in the world. For example: The Calendar of Babylon had 360 days ~ ALL pagan empires ignored the four extra days of "Remembrance for God" ~ which Enoch through Noah emphasized to all three sons were of dire importance. The pagan empires would all concoct their own make-shift systems for getting a 360-day calendar to come out properly, without remembering God.

360 IS A PERFECT CIRCLE

The calendars for the sun worshipping nations, are solar calendars, based on the sun, like the Roman Gregorian Calendar used today by the western world. The eastern nations, such as those of Islam or China, the calendar is a lunar calendar ~ for the moon, or for moon worship.

The Enoch Calendar worships neither the sun, nor the moon, it honors God. Further, it is the only calendar in the world truly using both the sun and the moon (as instruments of God) to bring in the roughly 365 days of the year properly. It has a special adjustment using the sun, and another for the moon ~ a harmony in which the holy days for God land on the same precise date, every year into infinity ~ from a mathematical perspective that is beyond astounding.

In fact, the signs of the Zodiac in every culture tell the biblical Story. They begin with Virgo the Virgin, and end with Leo the Lion.

There are eight planets (called "wandering stars" in the ancient world) moving through those signs of the zodiac ~ as if the stars themselves were a language ~ a language which tells different parts of a story from the different angles or dimensions one may look at them. As if the entire sky, and the eight wandering stars (planets) within, were but hands on a clock going "tick-tock" and counting down to something ~ as it were sands in an hourglass.

Enoch 40:2 And on the four sides of the Lord of Spirits I saw four presences (just as the name "YHVH" has four letters). 4. The first voice blesses the Lord of Spirits for ever and ever. 5. And the second voice I heard blessing the Elect One and the elect ones who hang upon the Lord of Spirits. 6. And the third voice I heard pray and intercede for those who dwell on the earth and supplicate in the name of the Lord of Spirits. 7. And I heard the fourth voice fending off the Satans and forbidding them to come before the Lord of Spirits to accuse them who dwell on the earth. 8. After this, I besought the angel of the Prince of Peace, who proceeded with me, to explain all that was hidden.

Jasher 7

44 And Nimrod dwelt in Shinar, and he reigned securely, and he fought with his enemies and he subdued them, and he prospered in all his battles, and his kingdom became very great.

45 And all nations and tongues heard of his fame, and they gathered themselves to him, and they bowed down to the earth, and they brought him offerings, and he became their lord and king, and they all dwelt with him in the city at Shinar, and Nimrod reigned in the earth over all the sons of Noah.

46 And all the earth was of one tongue and words of union, but Nimrod did not go in the ways of the Lord, and he was more wicked than all the men that were before him, from the days of the flood until those days.

47 And he made gods of wood and stone, and he bowed down to them, and he rebelled against the Lord, and taught all his subjects and the people of the earth his wicked ways;

and Mardon (later the called the Main god of Babylon, Marduk), Nimrod's son was more wicked than his father.

48 And every one that heard of the acts of Mardon the son of Nimrod would say, concerning him:

"From the wicked goeth forth wickedness"

Therefore, it became a proverb in the whole earth, saying:

"From the wicked goeth forth wickedness."

APKALLU

A set of seven "earthly (demonic) wisdom beings / angels" over which it is said (in Sumerian) that Marduk had charge, or interactions.

The sixth and seventh are: An-Enlilda, "the conjurer of the city of Eridu (Tower of Babel)." And seventh, Utuabzu, "who ascended to heaven (abyss)."

Jasher 8

The Number of New Beginnings

2 And when all the wise men and conjurors went out from the house of Terah, they lifted up their eyes toward heaven that night to look at the stars, and they saw, and behold one very large star came from the east and ran in the heavens, and he swallowed up the four stars from the four sides of the heavens.

These four stars seem to correspond with the four angels found in Enoch 40. The four sides are North (towards the heavens), East (coming from the beginning), South (towards Earth and Hades), and West (towards the future). In Hebrew, time and distance are the same thing. East is "the direction of the rising sun." Therefore, a star from the East is "something to come."

The Large Star can only be the "Elect One" sent by the Lord of Spirits found in Enoch 40 in connection with the praise and worship of the "four stars." In other words, Jesus is the "Large Star" on the horizon like the "sun rising" to come that the sages saw. Or, the "seed of righteousness" ~ the linage through which the king would come, which starts with Abraham.

3 And all the wise men of Nimrod and his (Demon) conjurors were astonished at the sight of the sign in stars over the Child born, and the sages understood this matter, and they knew its importance.

These "wise men / conjurors / sages" seem to correspond with the Sumerian "Apkallu." Though deified as gods, these "Apkallu" appear to originallybe priests and conjurors of Nimrod, just as the Book of Jasher indicates. The word Apkallu means the "the wise" or "sage." Seven Apkallu sages are listed in the "Uruk List of King and Sages"; but, greater still, the "wisdom of the sages" is said to be before Marduk (Nimrod's deified son Mardon), and also Enki (Satan/Saturn) the god of the Ziggurat of Eridu (Tower of Babel). Seven main Apkallu is a common theme in Sumerian writings. They are the dead or fallen spirits behind the conjurors and kings of Sumeria (where Nimrod ruled).

Ur is the Birthplace of Abraham.

Ancient Ziggurat of Ur

It is located by Eridu and Uruk.

Here is an Apkallu wearing the fish mouthed mitre from the city of Nimrud, in the Nineveh plains.

Uanna (Iannna) "who finished the plans for heaven and earth (Temple of Eanna)" ~ is listed as the first of these Seven Apkallu Sages, also called Ham's favorite granddaughter and Ishtar. She was born the claimed fertility goddess of the "fish egg."

She birthed the holiday Easter, the rabbit and the egg as symbols of fertility. And Lent, for the 40 days she cried for Tammuz.

APKALLU

CLAIMED WISE "GOD SAGES" HOLDING THE PINECONE (THIRD-EYE) WHOSE HEAD CAN BE INTERCHANGEABLE IN ART WITH THE MIND OF THE CROW.

In the "Uruk List of Kings and Sages," it says: "During the reign of Enmeduranki, the king, Utu-abzu was sage (right before the flood)."

"Utu" is Ham. It also means "ascended one." And, "Abzu" is the abyss where Enki comes from. This then is the deified version of the cursed son Ham appearing to claim he was everyone's advisor before the flood. Yeah, right... thief... It is the spirit working through Ham making these claims.

(continued) "After the flood, during the reign of Enmerkar (Nimrod), the king, Nungalpirigal was sage, whom Ishtar brought down from heaven to Eanna (Inanna's Temple)."

Then we have in other documents, Utu-abzu, is listed as the seventh (and last sage) "who ascended to heaven." This is following the sixth sage who: "was the conjurer of the (Enki) of Eridu."

In short, one of these Seven Apkallu Sages (the one claiming to bridge the gap of knowledge from one side of the Great Flood to the other) is "Utu-Abzu" ~or~ "Ham's guide."

These "Seven Apkallu Sages" of Sumeria seem to correlate with an evil version of seven angels of Enoch 20. These are the winged spirit guides of Ham, as he is copying the wickedness from before the flood.

So, Nimrod's family was actually trying to "become" and "copy" and call "themselves" God's most holy "seven," and depict themselves as "God's angels" ~ or at least claiming to get direct counsel thereby.

The reading could make one believe Ham died at the Tower of Babel. It states he went to "abzu" ~ the abyss/hell which he called "heaven" where Enki (Satan) is following the "conjuring at Eridu (Babel)."

ENOCH 20

1. These are the names of the holy angels who watch (and their roles).

2. Uriel, over the world and over Tartarus

3. Raphael, over the spirits of men.

4. Raguel, who inflicts punishment on the world and the luminaries.

5. Michael, over best part of mankind and chaos.

6. Sarakiel, over the spirits of the children of men that transgress.

7. Gabriel, over the serpents, paradise, and over the cherubim.

8. Remiel, whom God set over those who rise.

Ham was trying to copy, or claim he communed with, the same angels as Enoch (listed above). However, Ham's angelic Apkallu god-sages were simply the demons behind the priests of both Ham and Nimrod, later called "gods."

JASHER 8
Darkness sees its fate

3 And all the wise men of Nimrod and his (Demon) conjurors were astonished at the sight of the Sign in Stars over the Child born, and the sages understood this matter, and they knew its importance.

4 And they said to each other, This only betokens the child that has been born to Terah this night (Nimrod's head idol maker coming through the "blessed line" of Noah's son Shem), who will grow up and be fruitful, and multiply, and possess all the earth, he and his children forever, and he and his seed will slay great kings, and inherit their lands. The Child shall Destroy our Works.

5 And the wise men and conjurors went home that night, and in the morning all these wise men and conjurors rose up early, and assembled to Tell Nimrod.

12 And now our lord and king Nimrod, behold we have truly acquainted thee with what we have seen concerning The Terrors to Come through this child.

13 If it seemeth good to the king to give his father value for this child, we will slay him before he shall grow up and increase in the land, and his evil increase against us, that we and our children perish through his evil.

14 And the king heard their words and they seemed good in his sight, and he sent and called for Terah, and Terah came before the king.

15 And the king said to Terah, I have been told that a son was yesternight born to thee, and after this manner was observed in the heavens at his birth.

16 And now therefore give me the child, that we may slay him before his evil springs up against us, and I will give thee for his value, thy house will NOW be full of silver and gold for His Death.

In the Sumerian "twenty-one poultices" text the Seven Apkallu Sages of Eridu (where the Tower of Babel was) are entrusted with reading the "Tablets of Destiny" to the people ~ the witches that explain to the people what the "gods" want from their otherworldly tablets. The claimed "Tablets of Destiny" are magical documents belonging to the Enki (Satan).

In the Babylonian "Enuma Elish" text, Marduk (Nimrod's wicked son who had also become deified as a god) is placed over the 600 Annunaki gods (dead spirits of Nimrod's conjuror named Anuk). He controls mankind with the Tablet of Destiny, and the help of the Apkallu demon angels.

One can clearly see that not only is Ham's family copying Enoch's seven angels, except now as demons; but further, laying claim to God's Book of Life from Enoch 80 (new beginnings) and calling it their "Tablet of Destinies" through which they claim their dead souls control people.

7 Tablets of Creation
also called "Babylonian Enûma Eliš"

Beneath we see how dearly Ham (Utu) and Nimrod's son Mardon (Marduk) longed to be truly important. Clearly Ham (Utu) had taught his children to declare themselves as demon "gods." Text Reads:

80 Bel (Baal, also called Beelzebub) was the wisest of the wise, the sage of the gods. 81 In Apsû (the Abyss, Underworld) was Marduk born, 82 In pure Apsû was Marduk born. 83 Ea (Enki/Satan/Saturn) his father begat him, Marduk is now the god Nibiru (Jupiter).

Ham (Utu): The Thief and Liar

His family lived in shame & dealt in devils. Not only did he never go back and apologize to his father Noah, and return what he had stolen ~ but worse, he gave even greater lies to his own children. Since he is one of three sons, this corresponds mathematically with the one third of the angels having fallen. In short, Ham was the opening doorway for that one-third of evil angels on the new beginning of earth.

Enoch 80
7. And the whole order of the stars shall be concealed from the sinners, And the thoughts of those on the earth shall err concerning them,

Yea, they shall err and take them to be gods. 8 And evil shall be multiplied upon them,

Enoch 81
1 And he said unto me: "Observe, Enoch, these heavenly tablets, and read what is written thereon, read the book of all the deeds of mankind, and of all the children of flesh that shall be upon the earth to the remotest generations." And after that I said:

"Blessed is the man who dies in righteousness and goodness, concerning whom there is no book of unrighteousness written. 5 And those seven holy ones brought me and placed me on the earth before the door of my house.

101 'Mari-utu, Mari-utu,

"Mari-Utu" ~ is Utu (Ham) as the Sun God,

In the Global Flood Account of "Xisuthros," known from the writings of Berossus, a priest of Bel in Babylon, Noah (therein called Xisuthros) bows to Utu (his cursed son Ham) following the waters of the flood receding.
Another example of Ham twisting accounts. It is noteworthy that the Sumerian god Enki is shown as one and the same with the Greek god Cronus, the father of Zeus, in this account. Also, that the boat is claimed still intact in the mountains at this time.

Enoch 82
And now, my son Methuselah, all these things I am recounting to thee and writing down for thee. And I have revealed to thee everything, and given thee books concerning all these: so preserve, my son Methuselah, the books from thy father's hand, and (see) that thou deliver them to the generations of the world."

Jasher 8

Temple of Baal (Bel), Syria in image. Babylonians worshipped "Bel." Bel became especially used together with the Babylonian god Marduk.

31 Terah asked for three days to deliver the child. And the king hearkened to Terah, and he did so and he gave him three days' time, and Terah went out from the king's presence, and he came home to his family and spoke to them all the words of the king; and the people were greatly afraid.

32 And it was in the third day that the king sent to Terah, saying, Send me thy son for a price as I spoke to thee; and shouldst thou not do this, I will send and slay all thou hast in thy house, so that thou shalt not even have a dog remaining.

33 And Terah hastened, as the thing was urgent from the king, and he took a child from one of his servants, which his handmaid had born to him that day, and Terah brought the child to the king and received value for him.

34 And the Lord was with Terah in this matter, that Nimrod might not cause Abram's death, and the king took the child from Terah and with all his might Nimrod dashed his head to the ground, for he thought it had been Abram.

35 And Terah took Abram his son secretly, together with his mother and nurse, and he concealed them in a cave, and he brought them provisions monthly.

36 And the Lord was with Abram in the cave, and he grew up, and Abram was in the cave ten years.

Jasher 9

5 And when Abram came out from the cave, he went to Noah and his son Shem, and he remained with them to learn the instruction of the Lord and his ways, and no man knew where Abram was, and Abram served Noah and Shem his son for a long time.

Book of Jasher

The Book of Jasher means the "Book of the Upright."

Or, it could also be translated "The Book of the Correct Record."

It is an ancient documentary-style history of the world, going from Creation all the way through the Exodus.

It is NOT the level of scripture, but gives a fair and interesting backdrop on collections of events that those living at the time roughly perceived and remembered them.

It is recommended for reading in the Hebrew Bible in the books of:

Joshua 10:13

2 Samuel 1:18

I have found that the book does contain a few minor errors such as "Enosh" being translated as "Enoch" at one point. This is to be expected, as the copy it was first published from in Venice in 1625 was said to be barely readable.

There is a grand fight against the authenticity of this book, as with any book of Biblical significance. It is true that several "fake Jashers" have been made over time. None read or have the epic and genuine, nearly inspired feel of this document.

If it were a fraud, as some scholars openly against the book have claimed, then assuredly it could be easily called the most masterfully crafted fraud in human history.

The accounts in this book are also in the Midrash and the Jewish Kabbalah. This means that the accounts (including Nimrod & Abraham) were historical events known to the common man even in Biblical times.

That being said, in its transmission over the the years, it takes the later "Jewish opinion" on some matters. For example, speculating that Melchizedek is Noah's son Shem; for which I think the answer is larger.

No matter the case, it is a compilation of priceless Hebrew documents and records spanning from before the flood, through Shem to Abraham, then kept and polished into one complete history following the Exodus.

The Hebrews are record keepers, and their forefathers, the best scribes on Earth.

I believe, though with a few rough edges, that you are holding exactly what the title of the book claims:

A collection of documents preserved through time as the history of your world.

NIMROD

The War of Noah

Chapter five

Mt. Ararat

Little Ararat

Speaking of WARS of Noah and Nimrod, not only is it within the area of this very mountain that the oldest vineyards on earth are found ~ but greater still ~ seen beneath is one of the most controversial formations in the search for Noah's Ark.

In the *Epic of Gilgamesh*, Utnapishtim (Noah) was found while Gilgamesh says he went north from Ur and Uruk, towards the mouth of the Tigris & Euphrates. He arrived finally in the land between the two (mountain) peaks.

This area is called by locals the "Valley of the Eight."

Ancient Village of Kargaconmaz

Means: "Raven won't land."

Genesis 8

4 On the seventeenth day of the seventh month, the ark came to rest on the mountains of Ararat. 5 And the waters continued to recede until the tenth month, and on the first day of the tenth month, the tops of the mountains became visible.

6 After forty days Noah opened the window he had made in the ark 7 and sent out a raven. It kept flying back and forth until the waters had dried up from the earth.

8 Then Noah sent out a dove.

One of nearly several dozen strange stones that clearly had significance to early Christians leading towards the formation on the left.

Some point out they look strangely like giant ancient boat anchor stones. Others say they were for star gazing and later pagan worship? Perhaps both?

This one has become fused with the ground and has an ancient & mysterious Tower of Babel on it.

Durupinar Site

A mysterious anomaly that some call merely a wild geological "coincidence" ~ whilst others point out has the exact dimensions and shape of a "ground impression" of Noah's Ark?

EPIC OF GILGAMESH
Tablet Ten

I am Gilgamesh, and Enkidu (the goat-man) and I grappled with and killed the Bull of Heaven. My friend, whom I love deeply, who went through every hardship with me is dead.

Six days I mourned over him until the maggots came upon him.

Gilgamesh spoke to the tavern-keeper, saying: "So now, tavern-keeper, what is the way to Utanapishtim (Noah)!

What are the markers! Give them to me! Give me the markers!

If possible, I will cross the sea; The (only) one who crosses the sea is valiant Shamash (this is another name for Utu, or Noah's son Ham), except for him (Ham) who can cross!

Claimed "anchor stone" (one of many) from the "Valley of the Eight."

Gilgamesh describes a "wall of heaven" rock formation. Technically the ancient name for this mountain is "Place of Judgment."

The imagery of the Durupinar formation is provided by the Ron Wyatt Estate and Kevin Fisher of Ark Discovery. There have been unusually heavy fights against the investigation of this site. Whether this was the ark's resting place or not awaits further investigation. Either way, the area with this odd geological "anomaly" (which meets the dimensions of the boat as given in Genesis) does carry the ancient name:
"The Valley of the Eight."

Accordingly, this mysterious "Noah's Ark shaped formation" appears to have been in an ancient mudslide which carried it down from the mountain above called:
"The Place of Judgment."

It is additionally just askew from the ancient settlement named,
"The Raven (Crow) Won't Land."

And, it has a spectacular view of the mountaintops of Ararat only a few miles away. "And in tenth month the tops of the mountains became visible."
~ Genesis 8:5

The formation was exposed during an unusual set of three (3) earthquakes in 1948.

EPIC OF GILGAMESH

Anchor stone from Israel

Artist rendering of anchor stones on Noah's Ark

CARAHUNGE STONES

These stones (above) come from another site across the border from the "Valley of the Eight" in Armenia. They appear like copies of the claimed "anchor stones" from the "Valley of the Eight" ~ yet it is clear ALL of the Carahunge Stones are made from common stone in the area. Just as some of the stones near Ararat appear as copies from volcanic rock.

Archaeologists have several different views on the Carahunge Site. One is that it has to do with astrological observations, Or, second, a place of "holy stones" for pagan worship. The probability is both speculations might be true.

The question becomes: What is the origin of the reason this design of stone structure became a "holy stone" (idol) for worship? And, also, why did these objects become of astrological significance ~ just as the "Bull of Heaven" (a "holy cow" like the Egyptian Hathor, and later "golden cow" the Hebrews worshipped at Mount Sinai) that was attached to worship of the constellations and the stars?

There are some 200 stones, and 80 of them have holes, at the Carahunge Site ~ which look like copies and replicas of the stones in the "Valley of the Eight," just across the border, in Turkey, at the base of Ararat.

Many archaeologists believe these "holy anchor stone-looking rocks" to be the precursor to Megaliths such as Stone Henge. And, that their origin begins in Carahunge, which is often called: "The Armenian Stonehenge" ~ which appears to be rock copies of the very nearby claimed anchor stones from the "Valley of the Eight," at the base of Mount Ararat.

This begs the question: Why were ancient people worshipping, and creating replicas of what look like giant ancient anchor stones in the areas around Mount Ararat?

In the *Epic of Gilgamesh*, we see the "boat-man" who takes Gilgamesh to Utanapishtim (Noah) having long discussions about "holy stones" that go on the back of the boat. Enormous sections of the *Epic of Gilgamesh* (on tablet ten) in the journey to Utanapishtim (Noah) deal with these "stone things" which appear of dire importance and significance.

(TABLET TEN) TO CROSS WATERS OF DEATH, GILGAMESH, THE FERRYMAN OF UTANAPISHTIM SAYS. (YOU NEED) "THE STONE THINGS."

"WHAT IS THE WAY TO UTANAPISHTIM? WHAT ARE ITS MARKERS! GIVE THEM TO ME! GIVE ME THE MARKERS!"

HE CLAPPED HIS HANDS AND HIS CHEST, "'THE STONE THINGS…' ARE WHAT LET THE BOAT CROSS THE WATERS OF DEATH."

"IT IS IN YOUR HANDS, GILGAMESH, THAT PREVENT THE CROSSING! YOU HAVE SMASHED 'THE STONE THINGS,' YOU HAVE PULLED OUT THEIR RETAINING ROPES! 'THE STONE THINGS' HAVE BEEN SMASHED; THEIR RETAINING ROPES PULLED OUT!"

"WHY ARE 'THE STONE THINGS' OF THE BOAT SMASHED TO PIECES! AND WHY IS SOMEONE NOT ITS MASTER SAILING ON IT?"

(TABLET ELEVEN) ~ GILGAMESH SPOKE TO UTANAPISHTIM (NOAH), THE FARAWAY: "I HAVE BEEN LOOKING FOR YOU (GILGAMESH SAYS). I THOUGHT TO FIGHT YOU, BUT YOUR APPEARANCE IS NOT STRANGE ~ YOU ARE LIKE ME! PLEASE TELL ME OF THE "GODS," AND HOW YOU HAVE FOUND (ETERNAL) LIFE?"

ALTAR OF NOAH

POPE HAS TIA-MAT SHAPED VATICAN CATHEDRAL

TIA-MAT
Ancient "creator god" according to the Sumerians. A "feminine" seductive serpent.

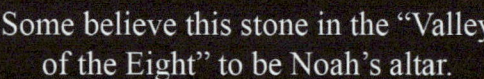

ENKI
Comes from Abzu

ENÛMA ELIŠ

Some believe this stone in the "Valley of the Eight" to be Noah's altar.

20 NOAH BUILT AN ALTAR TO THE LORD; HE TOOK ONE OF EACH KIND OF RITUALLY CLEAN ANIMAL AND BIRD, AND BURNED THEM WHOLE AS A SACRIFICE ON THE ALTAR 21 THE ODOR OF THE SACRIFICE PLEASED THE LORD." ~ GEN 8:20

80 THE WISEST OF THE WISE, THE SAGE OF THE GODS, BE-L (BA'AL) WAS CONCEIVED.
81 IN APSÛ (ABZU) WAS MARDUK BORN,
82 IN PURE APSÛ WAS MARDUK BORN.
83 ENKI (SATAN) HIS FATHER BEGAT HIM,
125 TIA-MAT (THE SERPENT) HEARD, THE SPEECH PLEASED HER,
126 (SHE SAID), "LET US MAKE DEMONS, [AS YOU] HAVE ADVISED."
127 THE GODS ASSEMBLED WITHIN HER AND GAVE BIRTH TO GIANT SERPENTS.
135 THEY HAD SHARP TEETH, THEY WERE MERCILESS...
136 WITH POISON INSTEAD OF BLOOD SHE FILLED THEIR BODIES.
137 THE FEARFUL MONSTERS SHE MADE THEM GODLIKE.
141 SHE CREATED THE HYDRA, THE DRAGON, THE HAIRY HERO (ENKIDU / PAN)
142 THE GREAT DEMON, THE SAVAGE DOG, THE FISH-GOD (DAGON) AND THE SCORPION-MAN (EGYPT'S KING),
143 FIERCE DEMONS, THE FISH-MAN, AND THE BULL-MAN,
153 "I HAVE CAST THE SPELL FOR YOU (MARDON/ MARDUK ~ NIMROD'S SON) AND EXALTED YOU IN THE HOST OF THE GODS,
154 I HAVE DELIVERED TO YOU THE RULE OF ALL THE GODS.
155 YOU ARE INDEED EXALTED, MY SPOUSE, YOU ARE RENOWNED,
156 LET YOUR COMMANDS PREVAIL OVER ALL THE ANUNNAKI."
(SONS OF ANUK)
157 SHE GAVE HIM (NIMROD'S SON) THE TABLET OF DESTINIES (THE TABLET OF THE CURSE SPOKEN OF BY ENOCH) AND FASTENED IT TO HIS BREAST,

Epic of Gilgamesh
Tablets 11 & 12 summary

Utnapishtim (Noah) tells Gilgamesh he sacrificed a sheep to the Lord after the flood. Noah tells Gilgamesh of the Lord, but Gilgamesh changes Noah's God into the Enki.

Just as many Christian artifacts (possibly even the "anchor stones") have been turned from the Glory of God to be twisted into the depths of pagan occult; you can see above the Vatican having turned "Jesus" into the Enki in the mouth of the snake.

Noah has Gilgamesh cleaned, and gives him seven (7) loaves of bread.

Gilgamesh, after hearing the truth, tries to get "eternal life on his own." He enters the "abzu" through a portal to get fruit from the tree of life.

A giant serpent steals the fruit.

Then, Gilgamesh decides (poorly) to summons Enkidu (Pan) from the underworld for guidance on eternal life.

This male/female snake and colorful false Tablet of Destinies to be worn over the chest plays a role in the end.

GENESIS TIMELINE

This timeline beneath shows the lifespans from Noah to Joseph as they are given in Genesis chapter eleven. This is the same chapter coincidentally which contains the fall of the Tower of Babel. As you can see beneath, the first few generations following Noah and his sons lived extrordinarily long lives. Shem, the one whom Noah placed the highest blessing on, actually outlived many of his most distant grandchildren.

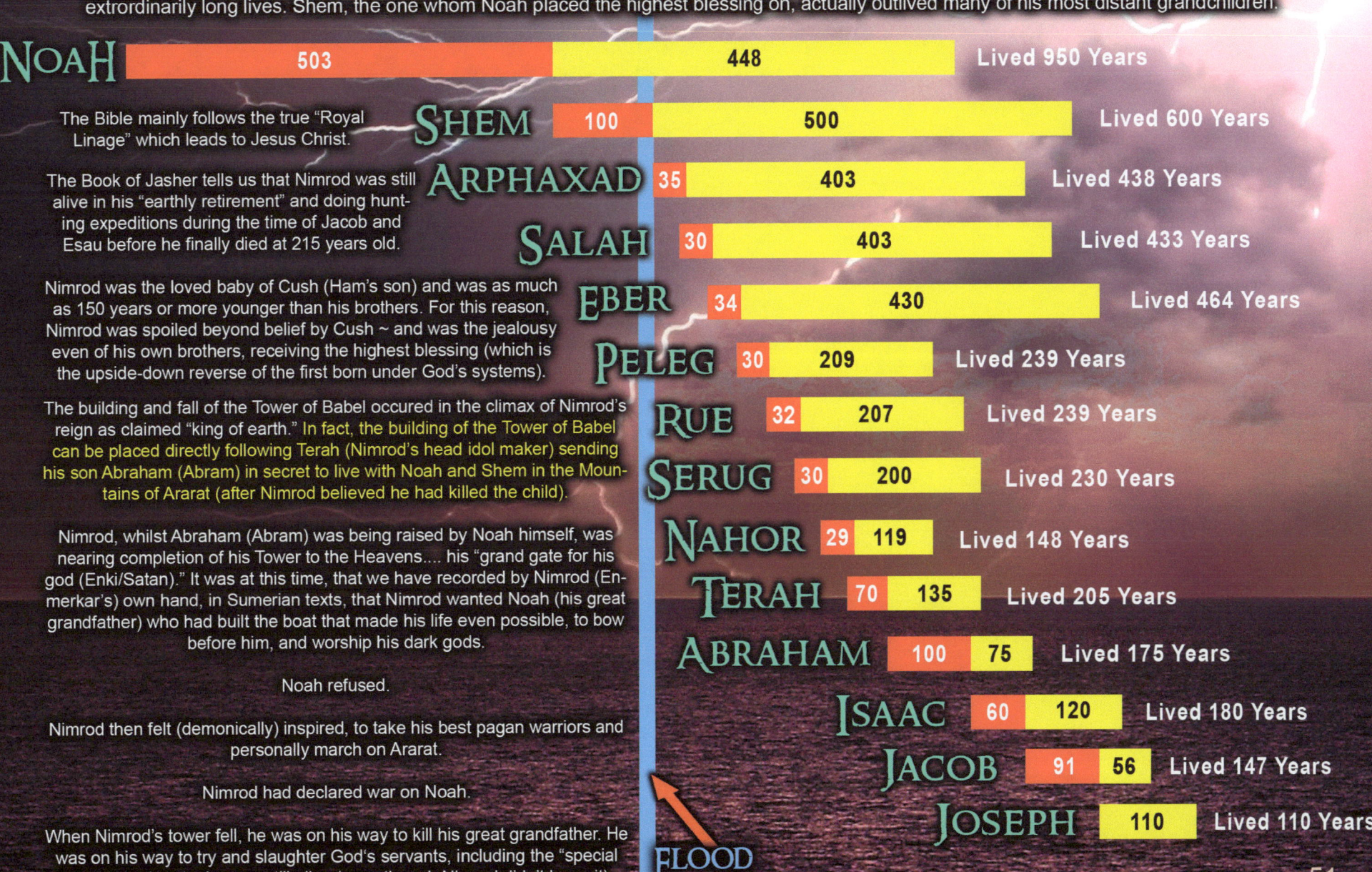

The Bible mainly follows the true "Royal Linage" which leads to Jesus Christ.

The Book of Jasher tells us that Nimrod was still alive in his "earthly retirement" and doing hunting expeditions during the time of Jacob and Esau before he finally died at 215 years old.

Nimrod was the loved baby of Cush (Ham's son) and was as much as 150 years or more younger than his brothers. For this reason, Nimrod was spoiled beyond belief by Cush ~ and was the jealousy even of his own brothers, receiving the highest blessing (which is the upside-down reverse of the first born under God's systems).

The building and fall of the Tower of Babel occured in the climax of Nimrod's reign as claimed "king of earth." In fact, the building of the Tower of Babel can be placed directly following Terah (Nimrod's head idol maker) sending his son Abraham (Abram) in secret to live with Noah and Shem in the Mountains of Ararat (after Nimrod believed he had killed the child).

Nimrod, whilst Abraham (Abram) was being raised by Noah himself, was nearing completion of his Tower to the Heavens.... his "grand gate for his god (Enki/Satan)." It was at this time, that we have recorded by Nimrod (Enmerkar's) own hand, in Sumerian texts, that Nimrod wanted Noah (his great grandfather) who had built the boat that made his life even possible, to bow before him, and worship his dark gods.

Noah refused.

Nimrod then felt (demonically) inspired, to take his best pagan warriors and personally march on Ararat.

Nimrod had declared war on Noah.

When Nimrod's tower fell, he was on his way to kill his great grandfather. He was on his way to try and slaughter God's servants, including the "special child" (Abraham) who was still alive (even though Nimrod didn't know it).

NOAH — 503 | 448 — Lived 950 Years
SHEM — 100 | 500 — Lived 600 Years
ARPHAXAD — 35 | 403 — Lived 438 Years
SALAH — 30 | 403 — Lived 433 Years
EBER — 34 | 430 — Lived 464 Years
PELEG — 30 | 209 — Lived 239 Years
RUE — 32 | 207 — Lived 239 Years
SERUG — 30 | 200 — Lived 230 Years
NAHOR — 29 | 119 — Lived 148 Years
TERAH — 70 | 135 — Lived 205 Years
ABRAHAM — 100 | 75 — Lived 175 Years
ISAAC — 60 | 120 — Lived 180 Years
JACOB — 91 | 56 — Lived 147 Years
JOSEPH — 110 — Lived 110 Years

FLOOD

ENMERKAR & THE LORD OF ARATTA

SUMERIAN ACCOUNT OF NIMROD & NOAH

NOAH — MT. ARARAT

MODERN IRAQ — TIGRIS & EUPHRATES RIVERS

ZIGGURAT OF ERIDU — TOWER OF BABEL

We are going to look at the elements and actual text of this Sumerian document. In order to do that properly, we have to understand some things about Sumerian.

First, this is the longest set of Sumerian "epics" (stories about the king Enmerkar/Nimrod). So, this was of the MOST EXTREME IMPORTANCE to the empire, and to the tower being built in Eridu.

It is a set of letters wherein the self-proclaimed "king of all earth" Enmerkar (Nimrod) is sending what he claims is his "finest messenger" from the area of Eridu to someone of grand "spiritual importance" in the mountains of Ararat. Even the messenger records that he is moving "fast as the wind" to cross mountain ranges and lands to carry Nimrod's messages and bring back Lord Aratta's replies.

In the first letter, titled "Enmerkar and the Lord of Aratta," Enmerkar goes to GREAT LENGTHS to express that he is the builder (or finisher) of the grand city of Uruk, one of the sons (the chosen son) in the linage of Utu (Ham), the great and powerful "king of earth," with much wealth, prosper, gold, silver and fine things, and finally that he is building a temple and tower in Eridu that he (Enmerkar) claims will "connect heaven to earth."

In short, it reads as if this self-proclaimed "king of all earth" (Enmerkar) feels desperate to both impress and get approval from the Lord of Aratta. Yet, even in that desire to impress, Enmerkar comes across as possibly the most arrogant, puffed-up & evil man alive ~ a ROYAL NIMROD.

ANCIENT ZIGGURAT OF UR

NEXT TO ERIDU

Trey's Notes: Imagine you took the time to write someone a lengthy message about all you felt you had accomplished, and you laid out your life's work (from your view) in your most eloquent writing. Then imagine it takes weeks, or longer, each time after carefully crafting each message, to get a reply from someone you are dearly seeking (or needing) approval from.

Then, when you get the reply each time ~ in response to your many pages of well-crafted words ~ and you are counting the seconds for the response, it reads something like: "What has any of that got to with me? What do I care what your master (the claimed 'king of earth') who sent you does?"

This is EXACTLY how these messages from Nimrod to Noah read.

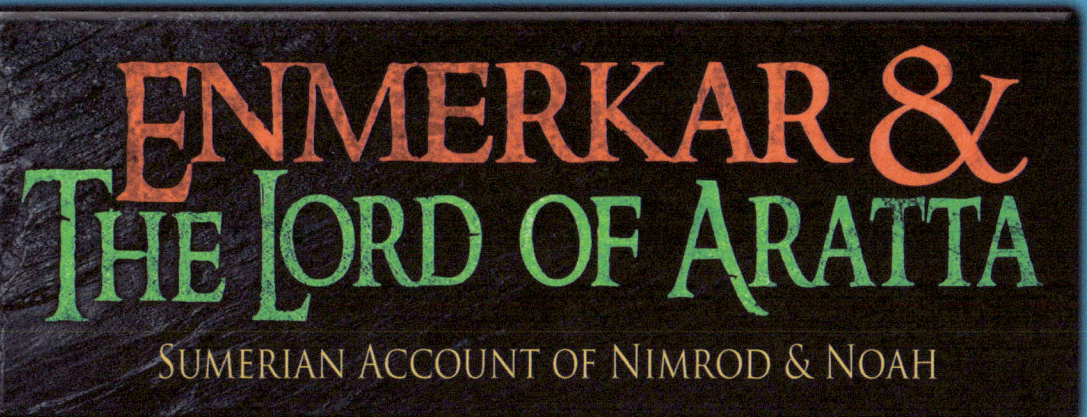

Chapter Six

We are going to analyze in this chapter letters going from the most powerful "King of Earth" to the most covered person he ever wrote to: The Lord of Aratta.

Mount Ararat in image

ENMERKAR & THE LORD OF ARATTA

SUMERIAN ACCOUNT OF NIMROD & NOAH

UR ZIGGURAT
MANY TIMES SMALLER THAN ERIDU BEFORE IT FELL

Scholars and historians have speculated for years on the identity of this mysterious person called the "Lord of Aratta," who Enmerkar was writing to, then trying to kill.

I will submit to your hands that the simplest answer is generally the correct one.

Like many occult texts, and even leading to your politics of today, this ancient document starts with the pagans telling each other how "glorious" and "(un)holy" they are. Both Enmerkar, then his wife (who is also his sister) Inanna praise each other as "gods" and "goddesses" of earth with power to do as they will, including to kill and destroy.

ENMERKAR/NIMROD BEGINS: "LORD ARATTA DID NOT BUILD FOR THE HOLY INANNA (HIS WIFE AND SISTER) -- LET ARATTA BUILD A TEMPLE BROUGHT DOWN FROM HEAVEN -- YOUR PLACE OF WORSHIP, AS THE SHRINE E-ANA (TEMPLE OF INANNA), THE HOLY PLACE, THE BRICK-BUILT KULABA (CITY OF URUK)."

Trey's Notes: Nimrod is starting by saying Noah, and a group of people living in the Ararat mountains with him, have not helped him build his pagan worship sites. Nimrod is upset about this. Now, Nimrod wants a giant pagan tower.

LET ARATTA SKILLFULLY FASHION THE INTERIOR OF THE HOLY JIPAR (THE PAGAN TEMPLE), YOUR (ENKI/SATAN'S) ABODE; MAY I (NIMROD/ENMERKAR), THE RADIANT YOUTH (HE SAYS THIS BECAUSE HE IS FAR YOUNGER THAN NOAH AND FEELS ENTITLED BECAUSE HE HAS THE STOLEN GARMENTS THAT ONCE BELONGED TO NOAH), MAY I BE EMBRACED THERE BY YOU (HE WANTS TO INTIMATELY EMBRACE HIS SISTER INANNA IN THE INNER CHAMBER OF THE EVIL TEMPLE HE WANTS NOAH TO HELP BUILD). LET ARATTA (NOAH) SUBMIT BENEATH THE YOKE OF URUK (MAY NOAH BOW TO NIMROD). LET THE PEOPLE OF ARATTA BRING DOWN FOR ME THE MOUNTAIN STONES FROM THEIR MOUNTAIN, TO BUILD THE GREAT SHRINE FOR ME, ERECT THE GREAT ABODE FOR ME, MAKE THE GREAT ABODE, THE ABODE OF THE GODS, MAKE ME FAMOUS, MAKE ME PROSPER, MAKE THE ABZU (ABZU MEANS ABYSS / THE UNDERWORLD OF THE ENKI) GROW FOR ME LIKE A HOLY MOUNTAIN.

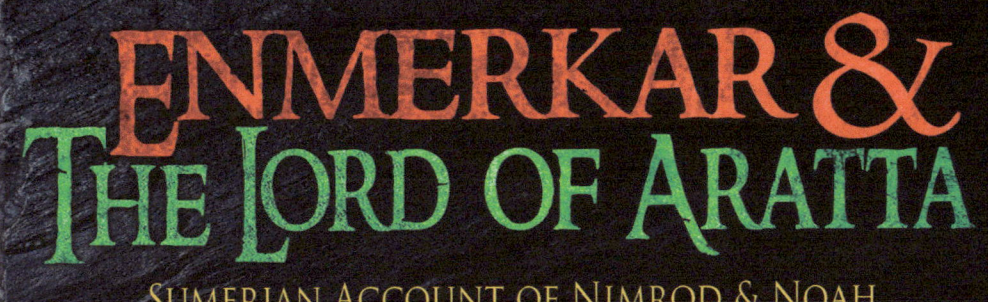

ENMERKAR & THE LORD OF ARATTA
SUMERIAN ACCOUNT OF NIMROD & NOAH

Trey's Notes: Nimrod is demanding that his great grandfather (Noah) now worship him, his gods, and help build his new "mountain sized" temple in Eridu (Babel). It is to be noted that his sister (who is also his main wife) Inanna is a giant player in stirring up the problems and demands he is now giving Noah, who was peacefully living in the mountains.

Thereupon the splendor of holy An (DEMON GOD OF HEAVEN), the lady of the mountains, the wise goddess, Inanna, the lady of all the lands, called to Enmerkar the son (IN THE LINAGE) of Utu (HAM):

(NOW INANNA BEGINS SPEAKING) "Come, Enmerkar! I shall offer you advice: let my counsel be heeded. Choose from the troops as a messenger one who is eloquent of speech and endowed with endurance. He shall carry the important message of wise Inanna. Let the lands the messenger passes on the way to Aratta humbly salute the important messenger we send like tiny mice.

Aratta shall submit beneath the yoke of Uruk (NIMROD).

The people of Aratta shall bring down the mountain stones from their mountains, and shall build the great shrine for you (NIMROD), and erect the great abode for you, will cause the great abode, the abode of the gods, to shine forth for you; will make you flourish in Kulaba (URUK), will make the abzu grow for you like a holy mountain, they will make Eridu shine for you like the mountain range, will cause the abzu (ABYSS OF ENKI) shrine to shine forth for you. When in the abzu you utter praise, from Eridu, in lordship, you are adorned with the crown like a purified shrine placed on your head, the holy crown in Unug Kulaba (URUK'S TEMPLE).

In the place of Dumuzid (TAMMUZ ~ THE GOAT), the people of Aratta shall run around for you (NIMROD) like the mountain sheep, in the fields of Dumuzid. You shall rise like the sun over my holy breasts! You are the jewel Enmerkar (NIMROD)! Praise be to you, Enmerkar, son in the linage of Utu (HAM)!"

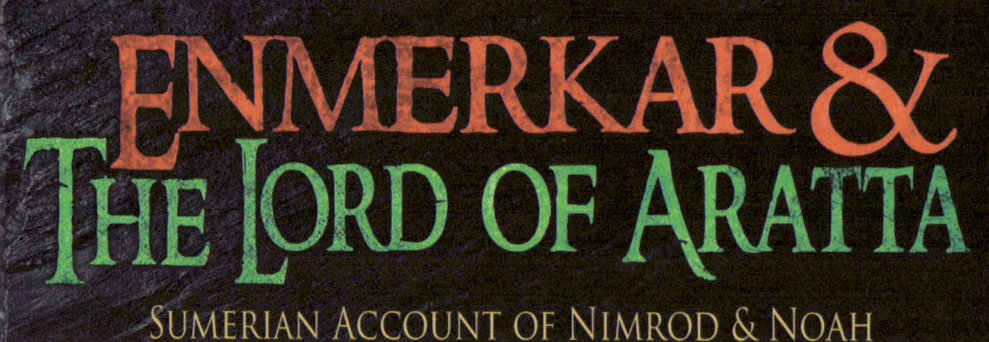

ENMERKAR & THE LORD OF ARATTA
SUMERIAN ACCOUNT OF NIMROD & NOAH

Trey's Notes: "Nimrod is intensifying the demand that his great grandfather (Noah) now worship him, his gods, and help build his new "mountain sized" temple in Eridu (Babel). It is to be noted that Enmerkar is calling together all the lands, who apparently understand each other's languages at this time, to be unified as "one tongue" for this "gate of the god" which "connects heaven to earth."

May Aratta pack gold nuggets in sacks for me (Nimrod). When I am adorned in Eridu by Aratta, may the people marvel admiringly, and may Utu (Ham, the wicked son who stole the garments from Noah) witness it in joy.

Trey's Notes: As a last instruction, Nimrod tells the messenger to speak a spell of Enki over Noah when he arrives.

"Chant to him the holy song - the incantation of Nudimmud (Creation portion of the Enki): "On that day when there is no snake, when there is no scorpion, when there is no hyena, when there is no lion, when there is neither dog nor wolf, when man has no rival (These opening lines read nearly verbatim much later passages from the Egyptian *Book of the Dead*)! The many-tongued, Sumer and Akkad -- the whole universe, the well-guarded people -- may they all address Enlil (Enki) together in a single language and a single tongue! -- Enki, the lord of abundance and of steadfast decisions, the wise and knowing lord of the earth, the lord of the wisdom of (the Tower of) Eridu, shall have all the speech in their mouths, so the speech of mankind is truly one."

Noah replies to all of this: "What is it to me what your master has spoken? What is it to me what he has said?"

THE WAR OF NOAH

Enmerkar and The Lord of Aratta
Nimrod
The Journey Examined

The text comes from roughly 20 Sumerian tablets. When it first published, in 1952, as a complete work by Samuel Noah Kramer (the world's leading Assyriologist in that day and a world-renowned expert in Sumerian history and Sumerian language), he immediately correlated it with the Biblical Tower of Babel account. Accordingly, Aratta is commonly agreed to be somewhere about (or surrounding) the mountains of Ararat.

Many would (and have) over the years also identified Enmerkar as the biblical Nimrod for other obvious reasons.

However, the identity of the Lord of Aratta is generally left as a topic of debate, or intellectually guessed to be some mystical character, or king lost to the sands of time ~ that Enmerkar (Nimrod) thought to constantly (and even desperately) try and communicate with.

These are the longest back and forth dialogs (done through a messenger) that Enmerkar (Nimrod) had with anyone, seeking blessing, favor and submission of Lord Aratta.

All of the dialogues and communications are instigated by Enmerkar (Nimrod) himself. They go from Nimrod expressing to Aratta how "grand and wonderful" an empire Nimrod feels he has built, to Nimrod becoming a clear family-feud style trouble-maker, and Lord Aratta largely wanting to be left alone in his gardens/vineyards.

In fact, Enmerkar (Nimrod) becomes incredibly concerned that the messages are not being correctly relayed by his messenger, as the replies are NOT definitely what he wants. Nimrod tells us this is the finest messenger in his whole kingdom. It is for this reason that Enmerkar (Nimrod) wants all messages done in writing on tablets that are to be taken back and forth.

Greater still, Nimrod claims that these very tablets were the invention of writing, an obvious exaggeration to show importance. What he is essentially saying (in his arrogance) is that: writing itself was invented so he could have this very dialogue with the Lord of Aratta ~ it is that level of important for Nimrod, and Noah could care less.

Ruins of City of Uruk, courtesy the US Army

Enmerkar and The Lord of Aratta
Nimrod
The Journey Examined

Thoth

Curiously, the Egyptian god Thoth was said to be the god of wisdom and writing with his magical tablets -- which may be a throwback to this very dialog between Enmerkar and the Lord of Aratta.

Whatever the case, this set of tablets is told like any Sumerian writing. It has magic, gods, and reads arrogantly with lots of embellishments to portray Nimrod in his "best light" (which is hard to do). Also, just as in Gilgamesh, if Utnapishtim (Noah) is sacrificing a sheep, Gilgamesh will tell us (in his version) that it is a sacrifice of a sheep to the Enki (Satan). Which is an actual example. Clearly Noah was sacrificing to God, not the devil. The same applies in this account.

Enmerkar is also telling us that these messages were of such importance to him that all the lands his messenger must pass through (which he owns and taxes) "bow like mice" (Nimrod's words) as his messenger makes his way each time to bring Nimrod's words to and from the Lord of Aratta (Noah).

It cannot be emphasized enough, that this story is being told to us by the Sumerians, from Enmerkar's perspective, and it has numerous versions (which probably got more elaborate over time).

Even despite that, in NO VERSION does Aratta actually submit to Enmerkar (nor give any blessing). He even goes so far as to say, that even if grossly outnumbered, he (Noah) would rather die than yield himself to Nimrod. Which is an important point showing the level of disgust and resolve by Aratta (Noah); and, on the other side, the very reason Enmerkar (Nimrod) is getting more and more angry.

It is true, however, that Enmerkar claims that attached to one of his messages he sent many large nets of what he describes as extremely fermented barley (beer). Enmerkar (Nimrod) firmly states that Lord Aratta was willing to keep the fermented barley (beer) ~ which sounds strangely like something Noah might do.

However, even after keeping the barley (for possible mountain brews), Noah was unwilling to submit.

Enmerkar and The Lord of Aratta
Nimrod
The Journey Examined

David & Goliath

Enmerkar then threatens to march on Aratta, in the midst of his projects at Eridu (Babel).

Lord Aratta (Noah), living by the mountains, clearly outnumbered, and whom Enmerkar himself tells us he believes is only a small community of people protected by "magical powers" (protected by God Himself), tells Nimrod's messenger that both sides should only send out their best warrior to decide the matter.

Aratta (Noah) is wildly outnumbered.

It should be noted that this is the first time in history that a battle is suggested to be done by both sides sending out their best warrior ~ as is the case in the story of David Goliath, and/or the Hebrews vs Philistines.

In response to Aratta NOT voluntarily submitting, Enmerkar (Nimrod) is red-hot enraged in violent fury!

Beneath is the exact response from Nimrod to Noah, directly from the texts of Enmerkar and the Lord of Aratta.

It reads:

"Aratta (Noah) is indeed like a slaughtered sheep! His roads are indeed like those of the rebel lands!"

(The messenger notes verbatim) In the brick built Kulaba (City of Uruk), Enmerkar (Nimrod) gazed like a goat... as if he were a huge snake coming out of a field he lifted his head. From his (Nimrod's) seat, he addressed the matter like a raging torrent:

"Messenger! Speak to the Lord of Aratta and say to him: (I have a very special garment) A garment that is not black-coloured, a garment that is not white-coloured, a garment that is not a mix of colours (Nimrod goes on and on about this "special garment" which presumably he is now shoving in Noah's face. In short, that Nimrod ended up with the garments that were stolen from Noah by Nimrod's grandfather, Ham/Utu) -- I shall give him (Noah) such a garment if he can win against me. My champion is embraced by Enlil (part of the god Enki/Satan).

I shall send him such a champion. My champion against his champion. Let the more able one prevail!" Say this to the Lord of Aratta (Noah).

Enmerkar and The Lord of Aratta
Nimrod
The Journey Examined

Second, (Continuation of Nimrod's demands of war upon to Noah) speak to him and say:

In his city, let his (Noah's) people go before him like sheep. Let him, as their shepherd, follow behind them. As he (Noah) goes (in shame), let the mountain of bright lapis lazuli humble itself before me like a crushed reed. And let them (Noah's people) heap up its shining gold and silver in the courtyard of Aratta for Inanna (Nimrod's sister and wife) the lady of E-ana (The Unholy Temple of Uruk)."

Third, speak to him and say:

"Lest I make the people fly off from that city mountain like a wild dove from its tree, lest I smash them (to their death).

And when he (Noah) goes, let him bring me the mountain stones (a reference to "holy stones" which may include the claimed "anchor stones.")

Trey's Notes: Enmerkar appears to believe (per the text) that he has had some of these types of "holy stones" delivered on a previous occasion. Again also, you do have sites in Armenia where it appears similar stones were manufactured, possibly as "fake replica holy stones."

And, let him (Noah) help build for me the great shrine of Eridug (Ziggurat of Eridu, Tower of Babel), the Abzu (place of the abyss where Enki dwells).

Let them (Noah's people) make its protection (the God of Noah's protection) spread over this land for me.

Lastly, recite this omen (spell) of the Enki (Satan) over him (Noah).

Enmerkar and The Lord of Aratta
Nimrod

Regardless anyone's opinion, even your greatest scholars of earth would have trouble packing more biblical appearing content into a set of three (3) demands than Nimrod managed to do in this section of his document.

Nimrod is referred to commonly (by his own words) with aspects of a goat, and also a snake. Whereas Lord Aratta, is nearly always referred to as a sheep, or shepherd of sheep. Even how Nimrod describes his plan to destroy Aratta (Noah) is by making Aratta "fly from the mountain city as wild doves" ~ a clear connection with the Noah account.

In the broken yet seemingly twisted and dark Sumerian account which follows, it essentially says that Enmerkar's heritage, through the line of Utu (Ham), was reared on the holy land of Aratta (by Mount Ararat).

It further says that Inanna (the claimed "moon goddess" who "grants desires") put on some type of "special white (or holy) garments" at her wedding to her brother Enmerkar. This could easily be interpreted as meaning the female portion of the garments God gave to Adam and Eve, which were passed through the generations, and stolen from Noah by his wicked son Ham (Utu).

Then, in the same context of these "white (or holy) garments" Inanna now wears, it goes on (at great length) to say that Inanna didn't steal anything from Aratta, sounding strangely like numerous paragraphs of spiteful self-justification. No matter the case, Inanna is very defensive about whatever "it is" she feels she has that was stolen from Lord Aratta (the shepherd of his sheep).

Inanna, after her rant of self-justification, goes on to say how the Dumazid (her goat-son, Tammuz) drunkenly dances and whirls around her with great joy about what is happening to Aratta (Noah). And that the Dumazid (Tammuz, the goat) is the "holy separator" of the people, the goat-man having selected Enmerkar over the people of Aratta (Noah). And that: "After the flood had swept over, Inanna, the lady of all lands, from her great love of Dumuzid (the goat Tammuz), sprinkled the water of life upon those who had stood in the face of the flood and made the land subject to them."

Then, in broken Sumerian, it reads: "The clever champion, when he came, had covered his head with a colourful turban, and wrapped himself in a garment of lion skins."

It then tells us Aratta was surrounded by darkness on all sides.

Noah was surrounded by the forces of Enmerkar and the Moon Goddess Inanna.

We have no record of Enmerkar defeating Aratta. And, assuredly, Enmerkar (Nimrod) would have recorded such on every wall of Sumeria if he could.

To the contrary, the first (and longest) portion of the story of Enmerkar and the Lord of Aratta, ends there. It ends with Enmerkar saying he is going to be coming to surround the "shepherd of the sheep" living in the mountains.

The next section (installment) of the Sumerian epic begins by portraying Aratta as having put some wildly powerful curse on Enmerkar (Nimrod) and his lands.

Therefore, we have no record of Enmerkar making Aratta fly off of his mountain like doves.

Instead, we have a record of Nimrod's largest building project (the Tower of Babel), and large portions of his army, being destroyed by the fire of God Himself.

Jasher 9

37 And they ceased building the city and the tower; therefore he called that place Babel, for there the Lord confounded the language of the whole earth; behold it was at the east of the land of Shinar.

38 And as to the tower which the sons of men built, the earth opened its mouth and swallowed up one third part thereof, and a fire also descended from heaven and burned another third, and the other third is left to this day.

39 And many of the sons of men died in that tower, a people without number.

Jasher Timeline

Abram goes to live with Noah & Shem in the mountains. He is sent there by his father Terah, Nimrod's head idol maker.

Nimrod believes he has killed Abram as a baby.

Nimrod begins work on the Tower of Babel.

The Tower of Babel falls.

Nimrod's empire is weakened. Greater still, the people disperse, and new settlements and enemies of Nimrod emerge.

When Abram (Abraham) is fifty years old, he leaves the care of Noah and Shem in the mountains.

Abram goes to visit his father Terah.

Nimrod does not know who Abram is, as fifty years have passed.

Jasher 9

And (after being hidden for ten years by his father Terah) Abram was in Noah's house thirty-nine years, and Abram knew the Lord from three years old, and he went in the ways of the Lord until the day of his death, as Noah and his son Shem had taught him.

And all the sons of the earth in those days greatly transgressed against the Lord, and they rebelled against him and they served other gods.

And they forgot the Lord who had created them in the earth; and the inhabitants of the earth made unto themselves, at that time, every man his own god; gods of wood and stone which could neither speak, hear, nor deliver, and the sons of men served them and they became their gods.

7
Abraham & The Fire of Nimrod

CHAPTER SEVEN

Jasher 11

1 And Nimrod son of Cush, the son of Ham, was still in the land of Shinar, and he reigned over it and dwelt there, and he built cities in the land of Shinar.

2 And these are the names of the four cities which he built, and he called their names after the occurrences that happened to them in the building of the Tower.

3 And he called the first Babel, saying, Because the Lord there confounded the language of the whole earth; and the name of the second he called Erech (Uruk), because from there God dispersed them.

4 And the third he called Eched, saying there was a great battle at that place; and the fourth he called Calnah, because his princes and mighty men were consumed there, and they vexed the Lord, they rebelled and transgressed against him.

6 And Nimrod dwelt in Babel, and he there renewed his reign over the rest of his subjects.

7 And notwithstanding this, Nimrod did not return to the Lord, and he continued in wickedness and teaching wickedness to the sons of men; and Mardon, his son, was worse than his father, and continued to add to the abominations of his father.

8 And he caused the sons of men to sin, therefore it is said, From the wicked goeth forth wickedness.

9 At that time there was war between the families of the children of Ham, And Chedorlaomer, king of Elam (this is the King that would put Nimrod under subjection, called "Lugalbanda" in Sumerian), Chedorlaomer went away from the families of the children of Ham, and he fought with them and he subdued them.

13 And in the fiftieth year of the life of Abram son of Terah, Abram came forth from the house of Noah, and went to his father's house.

14 And Abram knew the Lord, and he went in his ways and instructions, and the Lord his God was with him.

15 And Terah his father was in those days, still captain of the host of king Nimrod, and he still followed strange gods.

Jasher 11

Eleven is a duality. It can be prophetic or demonic. In Hebrew it often means disorder, transition, idolatry, or rebellion leading to heavenly authority. The 11th hour is one click to midnight; hell for some ~ salvation for others.

16 And Abram came to his father's house and saw TWELVE GODS (A DIRECT BLASPHEMY TO THE GOD OF THE UNIVERSE) standing there in their temples, and the anger of Abram was kindled when he saw these images in his father's house.

19 And Abram asked his father, saying, Father, tell me where is the God who created the heavens and earth?

21 And Terah said to his son, Behold these (Idols) are they which made all thou seest upon earth, and which created me and thee, and all mankind.

22 And Terah bowed down to his gods, and he then went away from them, and Abram, his son, went away with him.

23 And when Abram went to his mother and said, Behold, my father has shown me those who made heaven and earth, and all the sons of men.

24 Now, therefore, make me a savory meat, that I may bring it to my father's gods as an offering for them to eat; perhaps I may thereby become acceptable to them.

25 And his mother did so. And Abram took the savory meat from his mother and brought it before his father's gods, and he drew nigh to them that they might eat.

26 And Abram saw that his father's wood and stone idols had no voice, no hearing, no motion, and not one of them could stretch forth his hand to eat.

27 And Abram mocked his father's gods. And said, Surely the savory meat that I prepared has not pleased them, or perhaps it was too little for them, and for that reason they would not eat; therefore tomorrow I will prepare fresh savory meat, better and more plentiful than this, in order that I may see the result.

Jasher 11

Twelve is God's number of authority and government; exactly what is challenged in this text. There are 12 hours dividing a day, 12 months in a year, 12 primary constellations, 12 tribes of Israel, 12 disciples of Jesus. The twelfth Hebrew Letter is the Lamed ~ with a numerical value of thirty ~ its pictograph is a shepherd's staff.

29 And Abram took the savory meat from his mother, and brought it before his father's Twelve gods in the Inner chamber; and he came nigh unto them that they might eat, and he placed it before them, and Abram sat before them all day, thinking perhaps they might eat.

31 And in the evening of that day in that house Abram was clothed with the Spirit of God.

32 And he called out and said, Wo unto my father and this wicked generation, whose hearts are all inclined to vanity, who serve these idols of wood and stone.

33 And when Abram saw all these things his anger was kindled against his father, and he hastened and took a hatchet in his hand, and came unto the chamber of the gods, and he broke all his father's gods, except the largest one.

34 And when he had done breaking the idols, he placed the hatchet in the hand of the great god which was there before them.

Nabu

Idol of Son of Marduk. Nebo is in Isaiah 46:1 and Jeremiah 48:1. He would later become the Greek god Apollo.

JASHER 11

Eleven in Hebrew it often means disorder, transition, idolatry, or rebellion leading to heavenly authority. The 11th hour is one click to midnight; hell for some ~ salvation for others.

50 And Terah, seeing all that Abram had done, hastened to go from his house, and he went to the king and he came before Nimrod and stood before him, and he bowed down to the king; and the king said, What dost thou want?

51 And he said, I beseech thee my Lord, to hear me -- Now fifty years back a child was born to me, and thus has he done to my gods, judge him according to the law, that we may be delivered from his evil.

52 And the king sent three men of his servants, and they went and brought Abram before Nimrod. 53 And the king said to Abram:

"What is this work thou hast done to my gods!?"

39 And Abram answered and said, Not so my lord, for I brought savory meat before them, and when I came nigh to them with the meat that they might eat, they all at once stretched forth their hands to eat before the great one had put forth his hand to eat.

40 And the large one's anger was violently kindled against them, and he went and took the hatchet that was in the house and came to them and broke them all, and behold the hatchet is yet in his hand as thou seest.

54 And the king said to Abram: Do you not know the Power in the Room which you now sit? Do You think I am so foolish as to believe the story you just said? How foolish do you think I am?

56 I Do NOT know? How Foolish are you, my king? Woe unto thee forever

58 Dost thou not know, or hast thou not heard, that this evil which thou doest, is the Same as our Fathers before us in days of old, which caused the eternal God to bring the waters of the flood upon the whole Earth and destroy them all. Yet, you are doing the Very same things my king, and in your ignorance worshipping gods of wood and stone. So indeed, how foolish are you oh King?

61 And when Abram had ceased speaking, he lifted up his eyes to the heavens, and he said, The Lord seeth all the wicked, and he will judge them.

JASHER 12
You Shall Be Tested By Fire

1 And when the king heard the words of Abram he ordered him to be put into prison; and Abram was ten days in prison. 5 And they all answered the king saying, The man who revileth the king should be hanged upon a tree; but having despised our gods, he must therefore be burned to death, for this is the law in this matter.

6 If it pleaseth the king to do this, let him order his servants to kindle a fire both night and day in thy brick furnace, and then we will cast this man into it. And the king commanded his servants that they should prepare a fire for three days and three nights in the king's furnace.

7 And the king ordered them to take Abram from the prison and bring him out to be burned.

8 And all the women and little ones crowded upon the roofs and towers to see what was to be done with Abram, and they all stood together at a distance; and there was not a man left that did not come on that day to behold the scene.

9 And when Abram was come, the conjurors of the king and the sages saw Abram, and they cried out to the king, saying, Our sovereign lord, surely this is the man whom we know to have been the child at whose birth the great star swallowed the four stars, which we declared to the king now fifty years since.

10 And behold now his father has also transgressed thy commands, and mocked thee by bringing thee another child, which thou didst kill.

16 And Terah was greatly terrified in the king's presence, and he said to the king, It was Haran my eldest son who advised me to do this, which was a lie. Terah said this lie in order to deliver own his soul.

> I will bring that group through the fire and make them pure. I will refine them like silver and purify them like gold. They will call on my name, and I will answer them. I will say, 'These are my people,' and they will say, 'The Lord is our God.'"
>
> ~Zechariah 13:9

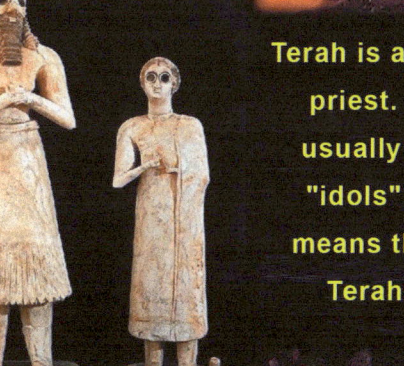

Terah is an ancient word meaning priest. The word teraphim is usually rendered "images" or "idols" but the word actually means the things pertaining to Terah, disgraceful things.

69

JASHER 12
You Shall Be Tested by Fire

Daniel Three

King Nebuchadnezzar made an image of gold, sixty cubits high and six cubits wide.

Shadrach, Meshach and Abednego told the King, if we are thrown into the blazing furnace, the God we serve is able to deliver us from it,

But even if He does not, we want you to know, that we will not serve your gods or worship the image of gold you have set up.

Then the King cried out: "Look! I see four men walking around in the fire, unbound and unharmed, and the fourth looks like a son of the gods!"

21 And they brought both the sons of Terah, Abram and Haran his brother (the father of Lot), bound & ready to cast them into the fire.

26 And they threw Haran in first, he was burned to ashes in moments when he was cast in, for his heart was not perfect with the Lord.

27 They grabbed Abram, and threw him in. Yet, he was Not burned, even his clothes were untouched.

And Abram walked in the midst of the fire for three days and three nights, and all the servants of the king saw him walking about in the flames, and they cried to the king, "Behold we have seen Abram walking about in the midst of the fire, and even the lower garments which are upon him are not burned."

28 The king heard their words and his heart was faint, for he was afraid.

32 And when the king saw that his servants could not approach the fire lest they be burned, the king called to Abram: "How is it that thou is NOT burned in the fire?"

35 And Abram answered out to the king: It is the God our Father, My King! It is The God of the heavens and the earth, in whom I trust, who preserves me in this flame... and who has all power, he delivered me from the fire into which your hands did cast me.

37 And the king, princes, and inhabitants of the land, seeing that Abram was delivered from the fire, fell and bowed down to Abram.

Seventy is the "Ayin." The symbol of the end, when all are tested by fire. For Light or dark, it means "to see."

38 And Abram said to them, Do not bow down to me, but bow down to the God of heaven who made you, and serve him, and go in his ways for it is he who delivered me from out of this fire, and it is he who created the souls and spirits of all men.

JASHER 12

39 And this thing seemed very wonderful in the eyes of the king and princes, that Abram was saved from the fire and that Haran was burned; and the king gave Abram many presents, and he gave him his two head servants from the king's house; the name of one was Oni and the name of the other was Eliezer.

40 And all the kings, princes and servants gave Abram many gifts of silver and gold, and many of the king's servants followed him, about three hundred of Nimrod's top men & forces joined Abram.

59 And (after the passage of several years) Eliezer, Abram's servant whom the king had given him, was at that time in the presence of the king, and he heard what Nimrod's vizier Anuki (father of the sons of Anuk, Annunaki) had advised the king, and that the king now intended great evil, and to cause Abram's death.

GENESIS 12

And the Lord said to Abram, "Go from your country, your people and your father's household to the land I will show thee.

2 "I will make you into a great nation,
and I will bless you;
I will make your name great,
and you will be a blessing.
3 I will bless those who bless you,
and whoever curses you I will curse;
and all peoples on earth
will be blessed through you."

4 So Abram went, as the Lord had told him; and Lot went with him. Abram was seventy-five years old when he set out from (the land of his brother) Haran. 5 He took his wife Sarai, his nephew Lot, all the possessions they had accumulated and the people they had acquired in (the land of) Haran, and they set out for the land of Canaan, and they arrived there.

6 Abram traveled through the land as far as the site of the great tree of Moreh at Shechem. At that time the Canaanites were in the land. 7 The Lord appeared to Abram and said, "To your offspring I will give this land." So he built an altar there to the Lord, who had appeared to him.

CHAPTER 8

ABRAHAM
THE FIGHT OF FAITH

Hebrews 11

1 Faith is the substance of things hoped for, the evidence of things not yet seen.

3 By faith we understand that it was by the Words of God that these worlds were formed, so that the things which are seen are made of things which are not seen.

5 It was by faith that Enoch was translated that he should not see death; and was not found, or seen anymore, because God had translated him. Enoch was not, for God took him. But, before his translation, he had this testimony, that he pleased God.

6 For without faith it is impossible to please God. He that cometh to God must believe that he is, and that he is a rewarder of them that diligently seek him.

7 By faith Noah, being warned of God of things not seen as yet, moved with fear, prepared an ark to the saving of his house; in the same hours for which God condemned the world. And Noah by having faith and trusting God, became heir of righteousness.

8 By faith Abraham, when he was called to go out into a place which he should afterwards receive for an inheritance, obeyed; and he went out, not knowing even whither he went.

Genesis 15

Abram trusted God, and it was accounted unto him as righteousness.

Before Abram leaves for the Promised Land, he must face the final issues of Nimrod.

In Genesis 12 beginning in verse 4 we are told:

So Abram went, as the Lord had told him; and Lot went with him. Abram was seventy-five years old when he set out from Haran (named after the land of his brother Haran, where Abram was living). He took his wife Sarah, his nephew Lot (Lot is the son of Abram's brother Haran who was burned in the fire), all the possessions they had accumulated and the people they had acquired in the Land of Haran (these would be the many gifts of Nimrod, and the 300 of Nimrod's best soldiers who had joined Abram), and they set out for the land of Canaan (what would become Israel).

Now, Abram was 50 at the time he was thrown in the fire by Nimrod. He was 75 years old when he (permanently) left the lands of Nimrod. So, if we look in the Book of Jasher chapter 12, verses 45 on, we find it says that:

And at the expiration of two years from Abram's going out of the fire, that is in the fifty-second year of his life, behold king Nimrod sat in Babel upon the throne, and the king fell asleep and dreamed that he was standing with his troops and hosts in a valley opposite the king's furnace.

And he lifted up his eyes and saw a man in the likeness of Abram coming forth from the furnace. And the king dreamed that all his troops sank in that river and died. And, the river turned into an egg before the king, ==and there came forth from the egg a young bird which came before the king, and flew at his head and plucked out the king's eye.==

ANZU BIRD And in the morning the king rose from his couch in fear, and he ordered all the wise men and magicians to come before him. **ONE-EYED**

And a wise servant of the king, whose name was Anuki (this is the magician Anuk, father of the Anunnaki, the claimed "gods of the air"), answered the king, saying, "This is nothing else but the evil of Abram and his seed which will spring up against my Lord and king in the latter days.

And behold the day will come when Abram and his seed and the children of his household will war with my king, and they will smite all the king's hosts and his troops. And that which thou sawest of the river which turned to an egg at first, and the young bird plucking out thine eye, this means nothing else, but the seed of Abram which will slay the king in latter days.

Why will not my king slay him now, that his evil may be kept from thee in latter days?"

Lugalbanda and the Anzu Bird

"Lugalbanda and the Anzu Bird" is the last of four (4) Sumerian texts dealing with the disputes between Enmerkar and the Lord of Aratta. In each text, Enmerkar (Nimrod) becomes more and more fearful of Lord Aratta (Noah). This is probably especially true since Abram (according to Jasher) is going back and forth to Noah's home in the mountains. And, Abram now has 300 of Nimrod's top military men.

Lugalbanda (as we have covered earlier) is the Sumerian name for Chedorlaomer of Elam, Nimrod's top prince and general.

Enmerkar takes what men he has and goes to surround Aratta, but finds it is now barricaded by thorns. Also, Enmerkar feels that Aratta, or those fighting for him, are letting dragons (or some type of dinosaur creatures) loose from areas in the thorns to attack his men.

Enmerkar (Nimrod) becomes very afraid of Aratta (Noah). His top military leader (Lugalbanda) sees Enmerkar's dismay as the empire weakens.

Lugalbanda has been raising an Anzu bird (which is the focus of this last text) ~ a raven-like giant bird with aspects of a lion that is claimed to be capable of flying away with a small calf. Lugalbanda believes this giant raven-condor-like bird is his friend, with special powers, and even helping him win against enemies, and guiding him from the air.

Lugalbanda, according to the story, has been with this Anzu bird since it hatched from its egg.

Lugalbanda may have interpreted Nimrod's dream as meaning he would be the one to subdue Nimrod, not Abraham. It is also hard to ignore the "one-eyed" symbolism in Nimrod's dream. As if the first Nimrod was a foreshadowing of the last Nimrod, the Antichrist to come.

Whatever-the-case, Lugalbanda believes the giant raven is telling him that he is to become famous, that there should be great idols of him all over Uruk, that he ~ Lugalbanda ~ should be the new famed ruler of the lands.

Lugalbanda leaves Enmerkar's side and goes back to Uruk alone. It is there (it appears) he has a romantic encounter with Inanna (Nimrod's wife). Indeed, she is the "lady that grants desires" for what she wants. Then, she gives him intimate advice on how to subdue Aratta.

However, according to both the Book of Jasher, as well as the Sumerians themselves, Lugalbanda ~ otherwise known as Chedorlaomer, the King of Elam ~ decides to subdue his own boss. He decides to go to war with Nimrod.

Noah never has trouble with either of them again.

~

JASHER 13

12 And in the tenth year of Abram's dwelling in the land of Canaan there was war between Nimrod king of Shinar and Chedorlaomer king of Elam (Lugalbanda), and Nimrod came to fight with Chedorlaomer and to subdue him.

13 For Chedorlaomer (Lugalbanda) was at that time one of the princes of the hosts of Nimrod, and when all the people at the tower were dispersed and those that remained were also scattered upon the face of the earth, Chedorlaomer (Lugalbanda) went to the land of Elam and reigned over it and rebelled against his lord Nimrod.

14 And in those days when Nimrod saw that the cities of the plain had rebelled, he came with pride and anger to war with Chedorlaomer, and Nimrod assembled all his princes and subjects, and they prepared for battle in the valley of Babel which is between Elam and Shinar.

15 And all those kings fought there, and Nimrod and his people were smitten before the people of Chedorlaomer (Lugalbanda), and there fell from Nimrod's men about six hundred thousand, and Mardon the king's son fell amongst them.

16 And Nimrod fled and returned in shame and disgrace to his land, and he was under subjection to Chedorlaomer for a long time.

17 And it was in the fifteenth year of Abram's dwelling in the land of Canaan, which is the seventieth (70) year of the life of Abram, and the Lord appeared to Abram in that year and he said to him, I am the Lord who brought thee out from Ur Casdim to give thee this land for an inheritance. 18 Now therefore walk before me and be perfect and keep my commands, for to thee and to thy seed I will give this land for an inheritance, from the river Mitzraim unto the great river Euphrates.

19 And thou shalt come to thy fathers in peace and in good old age, and the fourth generation shall return here in this land and shall inherit it forever; and Abram built an altar, and he called upon the name of the Lord who appeared to him, and he brought up sacrifices upon the altar to the Lord.

20 At that time Abram returned and went to Haran (the land belonging to his brother Haran) to see his father (Terah) and his mother, and his father's household. And Abram dwelt in Haran five years (until the age of 75). And many of the people of Haran, about seventy-two men (not including the 300 of Nimrod's top men), followed Abram, and Abram taught them the instruction of the Lord and his ways, and he taught them to know the Lord.

8 Covenant of the Pieces

Genesis 15

8 But Abram replied, "Lord God, how can I know that I will possess it?"

9 And the Lord said to him, "Bring Me a heifer, a goat, and a ram, each three years old, along with a turtledove and a young pigeon."

10 So Abram brought all these to Him, split each of them down the middle, and laid the halves opposite each other. The birds, however, he did not cut. 11 And the birds of prey descended on the carcasses, but Abram drove them away. 12 As the sun was setting, Abram fell into a deep sleep.

17 When the sun had set and darkness had fallen, behold, a smoking firepot and a flaming torch appeared and passed between the halves of the carcasses. 18 On that day the Lord made a covenant with Abram, saying, "To your descendants I have given this land—from the river of Egypt to the great River Euphrates."

Infinity

Trey's Notes: It was the custom of men to do contracts in this way, to walk between the pieces in a figure eight (an Infinity).

Not only does this passage begin in the eighth verse (New Beginnings); but God Himself (as fire) makes the Contract by Himself.

This means that even if Abraham fails in his end, God is keeping His ~ for His "Own Name Sake."

The Death of Noah

Jasher 13:9

At that time, at the end of three years of Abram's dwelling in the land of Canaan, in that year Noah died, which was the **fifty-eighth (58) year** of the life of Abram; and all the days that Noah lived were nine hundred and fifty (950) years and then he went to be with the Lord he served.

Nun 50 + Chet 8 = 58 Noah

Noah found favor and grace in the eyes of the LORD. Genesis 6:8

The "Nun" seen above looks like a seed of life. It is associated with the fish and represents fullness of life.

The five ("Hey") is the symbol for God's favor and grace.

The "Chet" seen above is associated with infinity. It is God's number of new beginnings. Just as there were eight (8) people on Noah's Ark.

The number 58 represents Noah. It is also precisely how many years after Abram's birth that Noah died.

"So it was in the days of Noah, so also shall be in the coming of the Son of man. For in the days before the flood, people were eating and drinking, marrying and giving in marriage, up to the day Noah entered the ark. And they were oblivious, until the flood came and swept them all away. So will it be at the coming of the Son of man" Matthew 24:37-39

MELCHIZEDEK
The Title Means King and Priest of Righteousness

Paul writes of the Order of Melchizedek in Hebrews 7:

7 This Melchizedek was king of Salem and priest of God Most High. He met Abraham returning from the defeat of the kings who captured Lot and Sodom and blessed him, 2 and Abraham gave him (Melchizedek) a tenth of everything. First, the name Melchizedek means "king of righteousness"; then also, "king of Salem (Jerusalem)" meaning "king of peace." 3 ==Without father or mother, without beginning or end, resembling the Son of God, he remains a priest forever.==

In Genesis 14:18, following the Rescue of Lot, when Abraham took "318 trained men (Nimrod's Men) and killed Chedorlaomer King of Elam, he brought the offering to this Unusual King, The First King of Jerusalem:

18 Then Melchizedek king of Salem brought out bread and wine. He was priest of God Most High, 19 and he blessed Abram, saying,

"Blessed be Abram by God Most High,
Creator of heaven and earth."

Trey's Notes: Following the Crucifixion of Jesus, several of his Disciples ran into an Unusual Stranger that seemed to know a great deal of the history and the Scriptures. They invited Him into where they were staying.

They Did Not Know who He was until the Moment he Took out the Bread and the Wine.

It was Then they could see the holes in His Hands.

For Jesus Christ to Ride into Jerusalem as a Returning King, This would need to be a King who had Ruled Before.

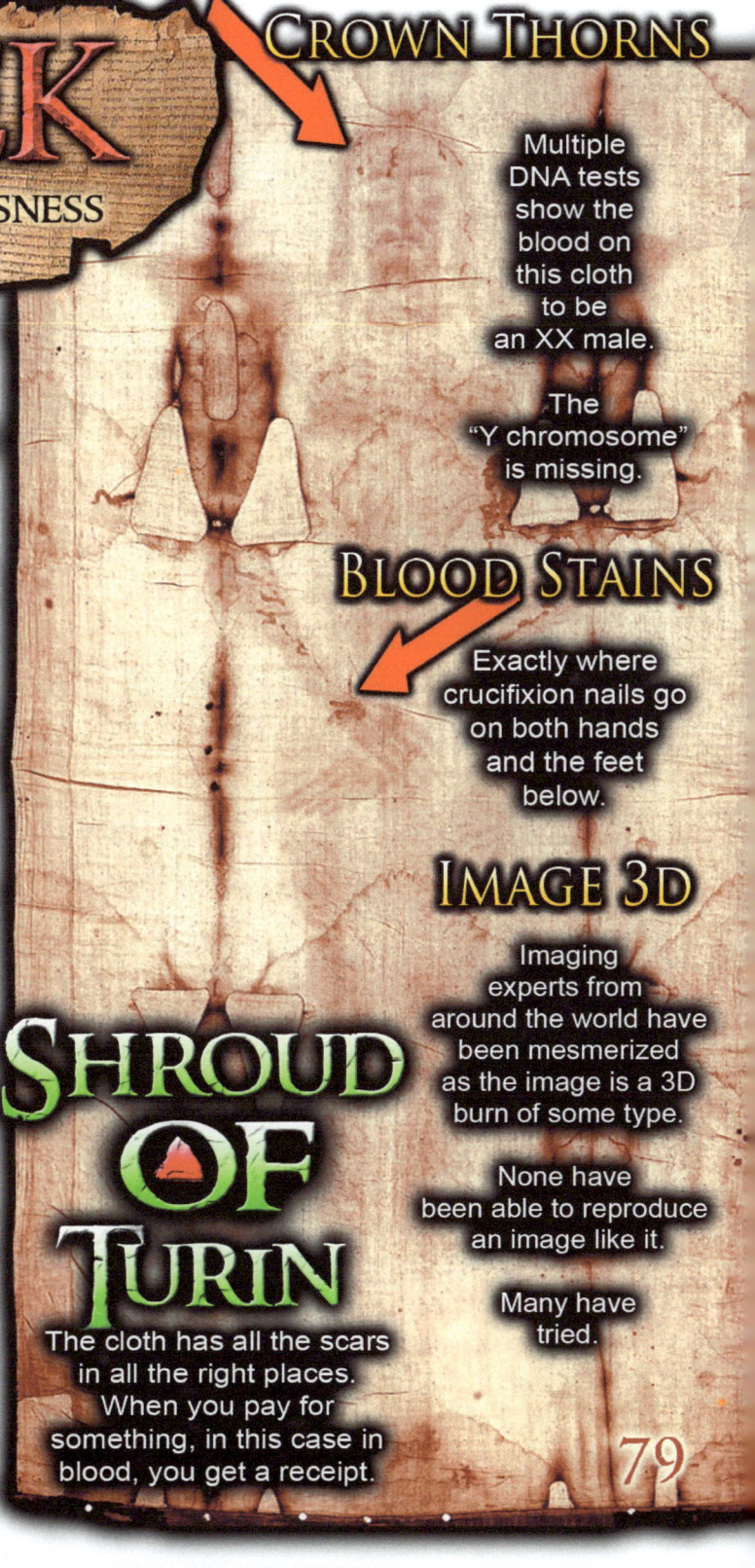

CROWN THORNS
Multiple DNA tests show the blood on this cloth to be an XX male.

The "Y chromosome" is missing.

BLOOD STAINS
Exactly where crucifixion nails go on both hands and the feet below.

IMAGE 3D
Imaging experts from around the world have been mesmerized as the image is a 3D burn of some type.

None have been able to reproduce an image like it.

Many have tried.

SHROUD OF TURIN
The cloth has all the scars in all the right places. When you pay for something, in this case in blood, you get a receipt.

Mystery of Melchizedek

Some believe that Melchizedek was Noah's son Shem. Certainly, there seems to be the hint of that possibility in the Book of Jasher. Or, seeming far more probable by the words of the text, someone very special that may have taken the reigns in the company of Shem, following the passing of Noah. A "Special Guest" in our broken world making an appearance in its opening hours following the flood. A- Mystery indeed.

And, strangely, the word "Shem" itself means "Name." The Hebrews take the word "Shem" to be the "Hidden Name for God." The Shem.

Yet, Shem (Noah's son) appears to us by scripture to be merely a man ~ one of the three sons of Noah ~ the one upon whom the Highest Blessing was placed.

Conversely, this Melchizedek is called both the First King of Righteousness & First Priest of Jerusalem. That is a Very Large title for merely a man. There are only Three parties in the entire Bible that carry this title ~ Melchizedek, Jesus Christ and the Church through Jesus.

Therefore others, myself included, believe as what Paul appears to write, that this Melchizedek was an appearance of the Christ Himself.

Either way one turns ~ the Mystery of Melchizedek may be far larger than any of us know the full details of this side of Heaven.

A Powerful Character in the history of our world indeed.

It is written that Jesus was of the Order of Melchizedek ~ a Higher Order than the Levitical Priesthood. So, that would mean He ~ if this be Jesus, a friend of Abraham and a friend of Shem ~ that He set-up the very Order through which He came, and through which He comes again in the end…

Perhaps that prophecy may be fulfilled, "I am the First and the Last. The Beginning and the End. The "Name" that reins forever."

The Three Visitors
The One in the Middle is God Himself

What we know from both Genesis and Jasher is that Abraham took care of his brother's son Lot; out of respect for his brother Haran who died in Nimrod's fire. However, Lot got himself caught up in the ancient cities of Sin ~ Sodom and Gomorrah.

Following Chedorlaomer (Lugalbanda), once Nimrod's "top military guy," having turned on his master Nimrod ~ per inspirations he believed he received from his pet Anzu Bird (a giant raven) according to the Sumerian Text ~ Chedorlaomer (Lugalbanda) went and captured Sodom & Gomorrah. This meant he took captive Abraham's Nephew, Lot.

==Abram took Three (3) Hundred and Eighteen (18) men== ~ possibly the Three Hundred Top men of Nimrod who had joined Abraham ~ and he went to go rescue his Nephew, Lot.

Chedorlaomer was killed in a raid by night from Abraham's Three Hundred men. And, Sodom and Gomorrah also were rescued by Abraham, who took nothing of the Spoils ~ lest Sodom ever claim it made Abram rich.

As a side effect, Nimrod was also partially restored over Babel and Uruk as Chedorlaomer was dead. And, since Gilgamesh (Chedorlaomer's son) was clearly friends with Tammuz (Nimrod's son) it is likely that this may be when Gilgamesh began work on his "playboy" epic and recording his trip earlier in life to see Utnapishtim (Noah).

Whatever the case, it was following Abraham's stealth-like defeat of Nimrod's Top man, Chedorlaomer, that Abraham gave the Tenth of what he had to Melchizedek as an offering.

==Then, in Genesis Eighteen (18) the Three (3) Visitors arrive.==

The Three Visitors

Chapter 18 The Lord appeared to Abraham near the great trees of Mamre while he was sitting at the entrance to his tent in the heat of the day. 2 Abraham looked up and saw three men standing nearby. When he saw them, he hurried from the entrance of his tent to meet them and bowed low to the ground.

Ruins Sodom & Gomorrah
In the Book of Jasher

The entire area of these now ash limestone cities have many, many, many salt deposits that animals come and lick in the evenings.

Salt can be tested to see if it is the remains of organic creatures (such as people).

The salt of Gomorrah was once living things. It tests identical to the "salt remains" of those killed in Hiroshima.

Sulfur Ball

95% Pure Sulfur

They light immediately, produce toxic fumes, and black flaming sludge that can burn through metal in minutes.

Sulfur Capsule

Most of the sulfur balls are in billions of capsules, like grenades that rained down. These capsules can range from the size of your hand, to the size of boulders.

They were cities which would trap and lure victims into their limestone maze, rob you, rape you, and even keep you alive in cages for things to eat you while they tortured you. They took great demonic joy in it.

It is a picture of Hell.

It is also a foreshadowing of the End.

The Destruction of these cities occurred at the direction of God who met Abraham ~ and by the Two Angels at His Side.

Lot ended up being the Door greeter of the Sickest and Wickedest places on Earth.

God saved Lot because of Abraham. This means you can pray for the salvation of those you love even they are sitting at the door of the City of Sin.

What you see in the image behind is the actual ruins of Gomorrah.

It is located by the Dead Sea in Modern day Israel.

Shem
The Descent Line

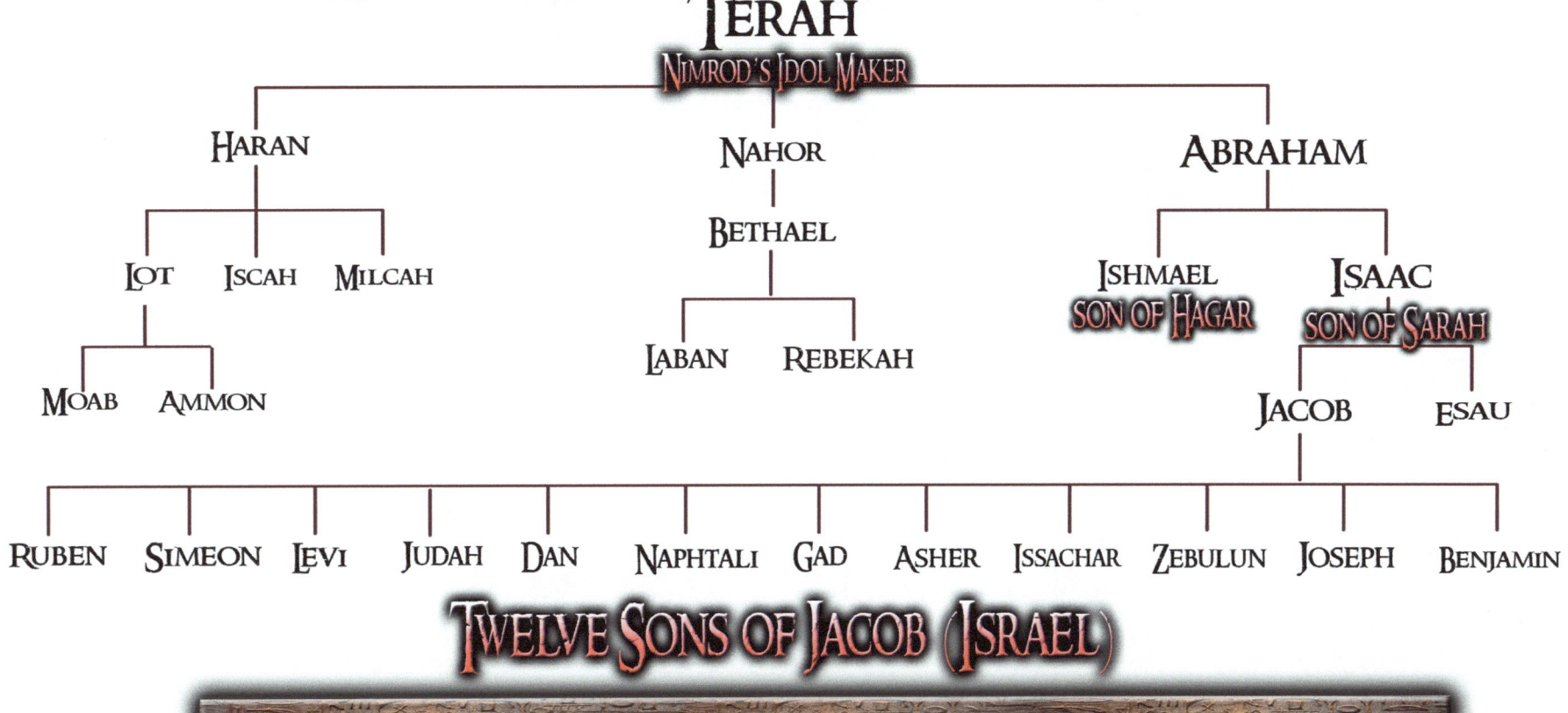

Twelve Sons of Jacob (Israel)

Jacob is who God would rename "Israel." He bought his older brother Esau's "Birthright" for a bowl of warm soup, as Esau did not respect the birthright. However, for the rest of his life Esau was jealous this had happened as he did not actually expect his brother to get the birthright from his father Isaac. So, Jacob (the younger of the two twins as he came out behind Esau) got the blessing.

Esau was angry and murderous about this his whole life. He intended to go kill his brother Jacob. But, an Angel of the Lord appeared to Esau on the same night Jacob's name was changed by God to "Israel."

When the two met, Jacob very was afraid. Yet his brother, with an army of four hundred men, ran and embraced Jacob ~ and both wept.

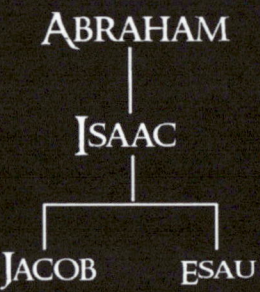

Death of Nimrod

Jasher 27

1 And Esau, the son of Isaac, the son of Abraham frequently went in the field to hunt.

2 And Nimrod king of Babel, also frequently went with his mighty men to hunt in the field.

3 And Nimrod was observing Esau all the days, for a jealousy was formed in the heart of Nimrod against Esau as he had become known as mighty in the earth. Esau is speculated by some to be who the Greeks called "Hercules."

4 And on a certain day Esau went in the field to hunt, and he found Nimrod walking in the wilderness with his two men, and Esau concealed himself from Nimrod, and he lurked for him in the wilderness. Esau was literally stalking Nimrod, the First King of Earth. He not only was hunting Nimrod, but wanted to kill him at close range.

7 And Esau leaped from his lurking place, and in a short struggle had stabbed Nimrod many times ~ then with drawn sword cut off Nimrod's head.

8 Then, the two guards of Nimrod ran forth. Esau fought a desperate fight with the two men that were with Nimrod, yet Esau smote them also to death with his sword.

10 And when Esau saw a cast of the mighty men of Nimrod coming at a distance, he fled, and thereby escaped;

yet, before Esau fled, took the valuable garments of Nimrod, which Nimrod's father had bequeathed to Nimrod, and with which Nimrod prevailed over the whole land.

Trey Note: Esau just took back the garments given to Adam and Eve.

And Esau ran and concealed them.

11 And Esau took those garments and he approached his brother Jacob and sat before him.

12 And he said unto his brother Jacob, Behold I shall die this day, and wherefore then do I want the birthright? And Jacob acted wisely with Esau in this matter, and Esau sold his birthright to Jacob, for it was so brought about by the Lord.

The Garments from the Garden of God

There are questions that have fairly straight forward answers, such as:

Who was the colorful and cunning serpent of Genesis 3:1–6 where Eve was tempted in all three departments of the human construct: The Flesh, The Mind and The Spirit...? As it was "Attractive to the Eyes, Good to make one Wise, and would make one become as Gods?"

The word translated in Genesis Three as "Serpent" is actually the word "Nachash."

And, the word "Nachash" has three uses in one: As a noun, it means serpent. As a verb, it means to be divine. And as an adjective, it means the shining one.

Serpent god from India. There are thousands of versions of these serpent gods found around the globe. Image by Pratheepps.

So, the "Nachash" in the Garden is a Luminous, Serpentine Angel ~ that apparently looked human-like, dazzling and wise ~ yet evil.

The Anzu Bird (Giant Raven) that was telling Chedorlaomer (Lugalbanda) that he should have Pride and Idols built of himself by rebelling from his own master Nimrod was assuredly the spirit of the same Nachash, and his world of Wisdom Serpents ~ as is written of the "Underworld" by nearly every ancient occult text from Vishnu, to Enki, to the winged serpentine angels depicted at the thrones of Pharaohs.

Ancient *Argentavis* bird at Los Angeles Natural History Museum. Similar to a raven or condor. The past is stranger than we imagine.

So, the question becomes: What were the garments that were given to Adam and Eve?

The Garments
from the Garden of God

Some have speculated over time ~ myself included ~ that the Garments may have been the sacrifice by God of a Lion; as a symbolism for the Coming King. Or, perhaps a Lamb.

That something innocent would have to lay down its life for the covering of sins, and as a foreshadowing of the Saviour to come.

And, it is certainly true that the blood of the Lamb in sacrifice was a picture of the sacrifice of the King of Kings on a cross, that would pay for the sins of mankind.

However, this would have been the first sacrifice. And, this is the first Sin.

In fact, this is the exact hour when mankind fell.

Everything was downgraded ~ from Adam & Eve to the Serpent (Nachash), to even the foods man and animals ate go from beautiful fruit given at no cost by God, to herbs and thorns from the sweat of the brow ~ the carnage of death in both man and beast starts in that very hour they chose the Tree of Knowledge of Good and Evil.

Let's look at the word "skins," and what may have been the case before and after the Fall. By merely changing one Hebrew letter, the "Alef" making the word "Light" ~ to the "Ayin" making the word "Skins" ~ something unusual emerges.

Some believe that "light" from God Himself emanated from (and as) the bodies of Adam & Eve ~ they lived in the realm of God and the realm of flesh.

When they ate of the fruit, that "light" stopped ~ they felt naked.

The problem was NOT their bodies, or flesh on the surface ~ but that the Light of God within no longer came through. They were NO LONGER what they were.

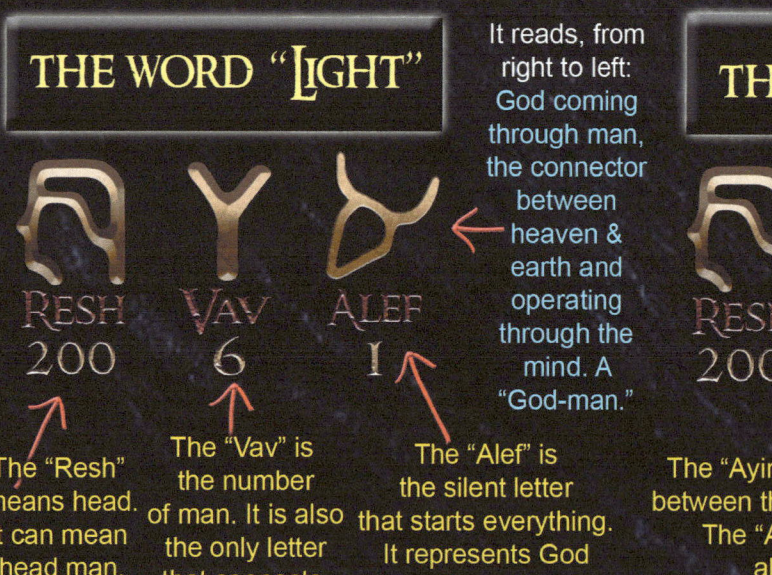

The Word "Light"

Resh 200 | **Vav 6** | **Alef 1**

It reads, from right to left: God coming through man, the connector between heaven & earth and operating through the mind. A "God-man."

The "Resh" means head. It can mean head man, or mind.

The "Vav" is the number of man. It is also the only letter that connects heaven & earth.

The "Alef" is the silent letter that starts everything. It represents God Himself.

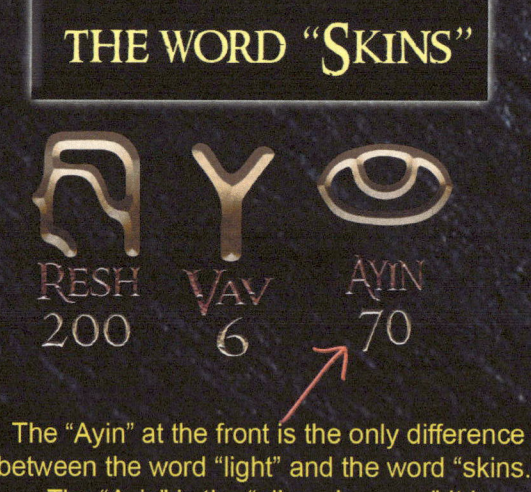

The Word "Skins"

Resh 200 | **Vav 6** | **Ayin 70**

It now reads, from right to left: darkness and light and the all-seeing eye come through man, the connector between heaven & earth. Darkness may now also have full reign through the mind of man. A weak "flesh-man."

The "Ayin" at the front is the only difference between the word "light" and the word "skins." The "Ayin" is the "all-seeing eye." It is also the symbol for the end.
It can be full of light, or full of darkness.

No matter the case, what we appear to see by the texts, is that those Garments made it back full circle from the theft of Ham (Utu) through the evil of Nimrod, to the hands in which they belonged.

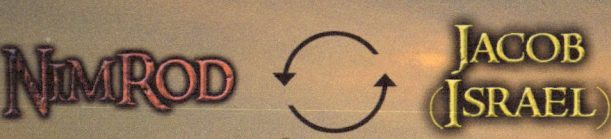

It was Nimrod that bragged to Noah of his MULTI-COLORED GARMENT.

It was Jacob who gave unto his favorite son Joseph ~ THE COAT OF MANY COLORS.

...which gave him pride over his brothers.

And, it was in the Tabernacle of God that the High Priest was to wear the Ephod; as God wanted a special garment made.

EXODUS 39

17 And mount on it a setting of gemstones, four rows of stones: The stones are a ruby, a topaz, an emerald. A turquoise, a sapphire, a diamond, a jacinth, an agate, and an amethyst, a beryl, an onyx, and a jasper.

7 Then the eyes of both of them were opened, and they realized they were naked ("Arum" ~ like unto the Serpent); so they sewed fig leaves together and made coverings for themselves. 8 Then the man and his wife heard the sound of the Lord God as he was walking in the garden in the cool of the day, and they hid from the Lord God.
~Genesis 3

Perhaps the answer of what "skins" these were may be found in the words of Ezekiel when God is speaking to the spirit behind the King of Tyre.

EZEKIEL 28

You were the seal of perfection, full of wisdom and perfect in beauty.

13 You were in Eden, the garden of God; every precious stone adorned you: carnelian, chrysolite and emerald, topaz, onyx and jasper, lapis lazuli, turquoise and beryl. Your settings and mountings were made of gold; on the day you were created they were prepared.

14 You were anointed as a guardian cherub, for so I ordained you.

You were on the holy mount of God; you walked among the fiery stones. 15 You were blameless in your ways from the day you were created. Until I drove you in disgrace from the mount of God,

and I expelled you, guardian cherub. 7 Your heart became proud on account of your beauty, and you corrupted your wisdom because of your splendor.

8 So I threw you to the earth; I made a spectacle of you before kings.

If these Garments were indeed the "Skins" of the Serpent Nachash; the Symbol of his shame, and sign of his orginal seal from Heaven ~ that would indeed make the Devil hate you.

Your priests, kings, politicians and Pharaohs of Earth have most all been giant "Nimrods" ~ believing their fancy clothes, jewels and elaborate garments made them special, or would save them.

Conversely, even if those garments were of a lamb or a lion, God Himself says:

"Obedience is better than sacrifice."

When all the while, just as for Nimrod, what brought power and riches over men ~ brought also the Great Curse of the Serpent.

To the contrary, to be a son or daughter of Abraham ~ sharing also in the promise and blessing of Abraham ~ has nothing to do with the color of one's skin, the fancy garments or clothes one may put on that skin, or the riches one may possess ~ nor the blood that flows in one's veins.

To share in the promise of Abraham; one must do as Abraham did:

"Abraham trusted God, and it was accounted unto him as righteousness."

But speaking of the Ayin (Ra) and worship of snakes...

The Journey Continues in

www.ingramcontent.com/pod-product-compliance
Lightning Source LLC
Chambersburg PA
CBHW041952150426

43198CB00004B/107